Last Chance
on
Earth

A REQUIEM FOR WILDLIFE

Last Chance on Earth

on

Earth

A REQUIEM FOR WILDLIFE

By

ROGER A. CARAS

Illustrated by

CHARLES FRACÉ

NEW PREFACE BY THE AUTHOR

SCHOCKEN BOOKS · NEW YORK

Clay said, as he stood before the specimen case, "Daddy, why does anyone
want to kill an animal?"

Pamela said, "Daddy, you would never
do that, would you?"

For PAMELA and CLAY

AUTHOR'S NOTE

THE TIME-LAG between the researching, writing, editing and manu-
facturing of a book and its appearance on a bookshelf creates an
unavoidable "fact-gap." The status of an endangered species is fluid
in most cases and even as we go to press we are aware of recent and
impending changes: the oryx herd is growing, the prairie chicken
has been given a new lease on life by the acquisition of land.

For the latest status report on any species of particular interest
we suggest you contact the World Wildlife Fund, 1910 17th Street
N.W., Washington, D.C. 20005 or the National Appeal of the
World Wildlife Fund in the country of your residence. Perhaps, if
you are concerned enough about an endangered species to write for
further information about it, you will want to include your check
with your inquiry to assist in the fight to preserve our wildlife.

Contents

Contents

Preface to the Paperback Edition

SINCE THE FIRST edition of this book was written in London in 1965, much has happened. There has been a growing awareness of the problems of wildlife. People who were only vaguely aware of the inroads being made into our remaining stock are now convinced. Laws have been passed in New York, Massachusetts, Connecticut, Kentucky, California, and Delaware making it illegal to sell the skins of endangered cats, wild canines, and crocodilians. (Word has just come through that England has also passed such a law.) We now have strong federal regulations in America. These are beginning steps.

None of the gains has been easy. Each step has been fought for. A law protecting endangered species was pending in Michigan when it was decided to pass it for the city of Detroit first. In that city, fur interests got to the Chamber of Commerce and were able to defeat the measure. Now, no law protecting vanishing cats from exploitation by furriers exists in Michigan. The fight there must start all over again.

The shoe companies in Massachusetts and upstate New York have fought against the ban on alligator and crocodile skins. In Washington there is constant pressure to pass control of endangered species from the Department of the Interior, where the experts are, to a joint committee of the Departments of Interior and Commerce, where the experts are not—and the exploiters *are.*

Early this year, the President issued an executive order banning the use of wide-spectrum poisons on federal lands in the ill-conceived program of predator control that has plagued North America for decades. Individual states and ranchers are working to find ways to circumvent that order. In Alaska, the fish and game officials have all but ignored the federal ban against hunting from aircraft and regularly issue special licenses to aerial hide hunters. Our wolves are still being shotgunned from the air.

The Humane Society of the United States assigned a zoo and wildlife expert, Mrs. Sue Pressman, to study the zoos of America. Her report, coauthored with the HSUS president, John A. Hoyt, will appear shortly. It will reveal very severe shortcomings in many American institutions. While zoos like the Bronx in New York, Milwaukee County, and San Diego continue to lead the way, many others are still operating like seventeenth-century menageries and contributing nothing to wildlife propagation and survival.

Recent news indicates that a regional commissioner in Tanzania has opened areas of Serengeti park lands to human exploitation. That means the area immediately adjacent to the Kenya border will be closed to the herds' migrations. Pleistocene herds that once migrated from the Serengeti plains up into the Mara Masai area of Kenya will be cut off and will, no doubt, vanish as a result. That fight is yet to be fought.

Not a month goes by now without at least one of the major national magazines in the United States carrying a feature on endangered wildlife. Whole issues of some magazines have been devoted to the subject. Books have appeared by the score, and radio and television talk shows report on the situation almost daily. There is anger, there is fury, there are running battles between federal and state governments, between the governments of different nations, between exploitative interests, between societies, associations, and individuals, but there is too little progress. There is some, that cannot be denied, but there is too little.

People hate each other and call each other names over seal hunting in the Arctic. Governments plan to start the exploitations of the Antarctic by sealing in that heretofore safe zone. Big game hunters, some of them, still pursue the polar bear by airplane and call people who object terrible names. Wildlife has become an international issue, but not enough progress is made.

S. Dillon Ripley, secretary of the Smithsonian Institution, has warned that between 75 percent and 80 percent of the world's principal wildlife forms could vanish within the next quarter of a century. The whales almost certainly face extinction unless the whaling nations ease off their slaughter, but people still argue slowly, as if they had centuries in which to make up their minds. In the meantime, the whales vanish.

It would be possible to run down the forty animals listed in this book—in its original edition—and update their status reports *in great detail*, but it would not be worth it. Too little change would be noted. Relying on the reports from the I.U.C.N., we can present a *capsule* summary of status as it is believed to be today:

ANIMAL	STATUS	DATE OF LAST STATUS REPORT
Arabian Oryx	"Free-ranging oryx probably number less than 200"	6/69
Florida Key Deer	"In 1949 the population was down to about 30; by 1963 it had increased to about 300"	1/66

Mesopotamian Fallow Deer	"A survey conducted in 1968 indicated that fewer than 30 appear to have survived along the Dez River."	6/69
Przewalski's Horse	"must now be very rare, to be numbered perhaps only in scores"	6/68
Cape Mountain Zebra	"a total of 130 animals"	6/70
Cretan Wild Goat	NO LONGER LISTED	
Giant Sable Antelope	"It seems certain that the giant black sable is in a phase of recuperation"	6/70
Javan Rhinoceros	"Critically endangered"	1/71
Pygmy Hippopotamus	"Very little is known"	6/70
Baird's Tapir	"dangerously reduced in number and very much in need of active protection"	1/66
Orangutan	"have declined drastically in the past hundred years"	1/66
Mountain Gorilla	"constant vigilance should be maintained"	1/67
Aye-Aye	"Possibly not more than about 50 specimens remain"	6/67
Spectacled Bear	"threatened with extinction"	6/68
Polar Bear	*Status confused but grave questions have arisen.*	1/66
Cheetah	*In serious trouble in Asia, situation confused but causing concern in Africa.*	1/66
Spanish lynx	*Populations now very, very low.*	1/71
Asiatic Lion	"at least 162"	6/68
Caspian or *Persian Tiger*	*Certainly fewer than 100 are left.*	6/68
Black-footed Ferret	"Endangered and on the verge of extinction"	6/68
Sea Otter	"Once nearly extinct but now recovering."	6/70
Giant Panda	"Rare, but not endangered"	1/66
Guadalupe Fur Seal	"Slowly increasing after having been almost exterminated."	6/70
Blue Whale	"probably the most gravely endangered of all the large whales."	1/66

Preface to the Paperback Edition

Tuatara	"existing populations are maintaining themselves satisfactorily"	7/68
Galapagos Tortoise	*All subspecies are in deep, deep trouble.*	7/70
Komodo Dragon	*In serious trouble.*	7/70
Eskimo Curlew	"perhaps nearing extinction"	7/69
Everglade Kite	"Excessively rare"	1/66
Monkey-Eating Eagle	"Probably less than 100 birds"	1/66
Whooping Crane	*Still seriously endangered.*	1/66
California Condor	*Still seriously endangered.*	1/66
Steller's Albatross	NO LONGER LISTED	
Hawaiian Goose	"Still very rare in the wild but in much better shape than in 1948 when the restoration campaign began."	1/66
Indian Pink-headed Duck	EXTINCT	
Attwater's Prairie Chicken	"Very rare and endangered"	6/67
Notornis	"Rare and localized"	10/66
Ivory-billed Woodpecker	*Situation confused but known to be desperate at best.*	10/66

And so it goes. Over 1000 species of animals in trouble and perhaps as many as 10 percent of the world's plants are going, too. There are those men, and some of them in positions of power, who either disbelieved all of this or are too incomplete to care. One thing is for certain, time is running out and history will soon have a completed file by which to judge us.

When given the opportunity to do a preface to a new edition of his book, an author has a chance to insert something he failed to say earlier. It is a rare chance to have a second "go." I will add just this thought—there is nothing man is now doing on this planet that cannot be corrected by time, save this one thing: the extinction of a single species is the one permanent change man is capable of making in the Cosmos. Think about that for a moment or two. It is very frightening, unless you like playing the role of a god. Personally, I do not.

ROGER CARAS

East Hampton, N.Y.
April 1972

Preface

THE SADDEST THING about this book, and possibly one of the most revealing, is the fact that it could not be written twenty-five years from now. The reasoning behind this admittedly strange observation is that this book is about forty animals that are or were recently in danger of disappearing. Twenty-five years from now, some, perhaps many, possibly even all of them will be gone. It will be quite possible in a quarter of a century, however, to write a book like this about forty different animals.

A second ominous note is that this book's content was perfectly predictable—indeed, much of it was actually foretold—twenty-five years ago. Nothing, obviously, was done in many cases; too little in most; enough in only a very few.

What, then, is the purpose of this book? Quite simply, it is a warning and an attempt to put man on record. This book, like many others, is a clarion, a horn, an alarm. Let the call be harsh! Let no one's nerves be spared!

Man, mankind, humanity, whoever and whatever you are, take note! Your ignorance can no longer be accepted in defense. You will forever live with what you do from now on.

Man evolved into his present form concurrently with a great many other animal species. Some that preceded him have lasted miraculously into our present era. Not a few come to us from times more ancient than we can readily comprehend. Man was and is a part of this whole vast, pulsing scene. He is legitimate heir to a natural heritage, he is an animal among animals—spirited, spiritual, inspired though he may be. His estate is the estate of rock, sea, and air, bush, fire, and earth. His stuff is the stuff of the planet, the solar system, and the universe. So it is with the worm, the fish, the eagle, and the swine. In this regard, at least, man is not unique.

But, we must acknowledge, man is a creature apart. For whatever reasons and by whatever means you wish to cite—speech, enlarged brain, opposable thumb, erect posture, omnivorous appetite, ability to adapt, toolmaking, weaponry, all of these and any of these—however you will have it, man is different. The difference that concerns us most here is man's unique ability to dominate and order his surroundings. An elephant can knock over a tree if he wants its tender leaves, but he cannot do it as part of a long-range plan and he cannot replace it with a hybrid of his own invention. Only man can reason: he knows what he is doing, knows why he is doing it, and understands both the consequences and alternatives. At least he should understand, for he has been so endowed.

Man cannot yet control the oceans' tides, the volcano, earthquake, hurricane, or polar icecap, but he can order his planet in a remarkable way. It is these activities that so drastically affect wildlife and reduce it in kind and number. It is man's disorderly ordering, his shortsighted long-range planning, and his thoughtless scientific genius that have brought about this near catastrophe—a near catastrophe not in the sense that it nearly happened but in the sense that it is nearly here. For it is coming; only a quality of humanity not heretofore evident in man's make-up will prevent it. Man's record so far, as the custodian of life on this one planet, at least, is bad, very bad indeed. Whether or not he can ever prove himself worthy of so awesome a trust is really our topic here.

There was a time when nature could evolve new species and reshape the fauna of a land according to the niches that were vacant or vacated, according, also, to the way the land itself was reshaped. This could be done because there existed adequate space, time, and raw materials. The space is now gone, bulldozed over, and forces other than natural ones play upon too much of our planet's surface. Time is gone also; man can eliminate most of the wildlife on this planet before natural forces can reshape them. For that reason we must acknowledge that the raw material, too, is going or gone. Nature can never again make a new kind of elephant, or anteater, or whale, not as long as man is around with rifle and steam shovel.

Without the possibility of a major species evolving anew anywhere save perhaps in the depths of the sea, and there only for a little while longer, we must attempt to sustain those species that have evolved in the past. The decision as to what is to die and what is to survive is ours to make, in this generation and the next. To a very large degree, the future of wildlife on this planet will be determined irrevocably before the dawn of the twenty-first century. We are about to commit ourselves once and for all time either to a planet rich in wonderment and beauty or to a planet that is a mockery of itself, drenched in poisons, littered with metal junk heaps, and stripped of timber, an ugly planet that will soon enough strangle itself on its own reeking gases and gag itself on its self-spawned contaminated juices. This is *mankind's* last chance on earth. From here on, the world will be a heaven or hell of our own choosing.

The Arabian Oryx

In the recent past the Arabian oryx, a beautiful desert antelope, white, chocolate, black, and fawn, lived and thrived in the sandy wastes and gravel plains of the Arabian peninsula, perfectly suited to a harsh climate and forbidding terrain that are inhospitable to many other animals. But the oryx, which survived the rigors of nature for millennia, could not survive the onslaught of man; in little more than half a century hunters have reduced their number so much that the species is in critical danger of extinction.

The slow but steady destruction of the oryx was originally the handiwork of local Bedouin tribes, who preyed on the elusive roaming herds to the best of their ability. The rate of attrition has increased with the quality of the firearms available. The greatest destruction has come in recent years, however, with the advent of motorized hunting parties from outside the area. In 1959, it was estimated that no more than eighty to one hundred specimens survived in Aden Protectorate. In December of the following year, a party of hunters equipped with desert cars and high-powered rifles raided the area around Ramlat Mitan for several weeks. Hunting from fast-moving cars and chasing down small herds on the flats, they killed at least forty-eight priceless oryx. In December of 1961, they came back and killed sixteen more.

British and American oil company employees hunted the beautiful oryx for years as an escape from boredom and as a gesture of defiance in a land both inhospitable and uncomfortable. The rulers of the area cared so little for the safekeeping of the natural heritage left them that they mounted royal motorized hunts and shot down whole herds of oryx with machine guns in savage and incomprehensible blood baths. The natives in the area, too, have contributed to the destruction; steeped in ignorance and superstition, they prize the flesh of the oryx because they believe that when eaten it will impart the alertness and swiftness of the animal and will expel a bullet lodged in the body no matter how long it has been there.

The Arabian oryx, *Oryx leucoryx*, once ranged over most of the Arabian peninsula, wherever suitable habitat was found. How far north the animal lived is not certain, but it was at least as far as the Syrian desert. Sinai, Palestine, Jordan, and Iraq once knew this handsome and distinctive animal. Since the species prefers the great sand seas in winter and the flat, almost featureless *jol* or gravel areas in summer, habitat destruction cannot be blamed for the fact that fewer than two hundred (possibly fewer than one hundred) specimens remain in this vast area. The rifle and the machine gun are the instruments which nearly destroyed this handsome animal.

The Arabian Oryx

Small populations survived until recently in two sandy refuges in Saudi Arabia: the northern Nafud and the southern wilderness of Rub al Khali. Rumors persist that specimens remain in the Jauf area of Yemen. In 1962, a herd of twenty was seen and photographed in an isolated area in Oman.

In 1903 oryx were abundant enough that the Bronx Zoo's purchase of a male specimen from Carl Hagenbeck, an animal dealer in Hamburg, Germany, for $725 seemed unremarkable. Six years later a dealer at Coney Island sold the zoo a female of the species for $175. The pair produced four young, the last of which died in 1925. Although these facts are in the records of a large and well-known zoo, like thousands of other statistics they went unnoticed.

The Arabian Oryx

In May, 1963, four Arabian oryx passed through New York en route to the Maytag Zoo in Phoenix, Arizona. This event attracted world-wide attention. Oryx were by that time so rare that the shipment required the cooperative effort of conservation forces and funds in at least four countries: England, the United States, Kenya, and Aden Protectorate. The World Wildlife Fund alone contributed $6,160 to "Operation Oryx" of the Fauna Preservation Society, which managed the project. Borrowed aircraft, custom-equipped capturing cars, trained zoologists, and game specialists were all needed. As a result of a major international effort, the Arabian oryx became the first nearly extinct mammal to be deliberately captured, removed, and established on foreign soil, not for exhibition but as the nucleus of a breeding herd. This difficult and costly enterprise was necessary because no force on earth could guarantee the survival of the oryx in its natural range. Man simply could not be trusted.

The expedition to Aden netted three animals and the London Zoo donated the fourth to form the herd nucleus. In September, 1963, the first calf was born. Since then further specimens have reached Phoenix from Bahrain and Saudi Arabia, and more calves have been produced. The new herd, far from its native soil, is on its way. If lasting political stability can be attained and a sense of conservation responsibility instilled, it may one day be possible to return a small herd to the animal's native land.

How go things now? The number of Arabian oryx in captivity stood at twenty-three in 1962:

Zoo	Males	Females
London, U. K.	1	0
Phoenix, Arizona, U. S. A.	3	2
Riyadh, Saudi Arabia	7	6
Rome, Italy	1	1
Salwa, Kuwait	0	2
Totals	12	11

By the end of the following year, according to the fifth volume of *The International Zoo Yearbook* published by the Zoological Society of London, the stock had increased to seventeen males and ten females; from twenty-three specimens to twenty-seven. The increase, from the point of view of percentages, was substantial. If the animals continue to reproduce at the same rate, the world-wide captive stock will number over a hundred and twenty specimens in the first ten years and should multiply dramatically after that. It is far easier to control the fate of a herd and a species in Arizona than it is on the unpoliced gravel plains of Aden.

The story of the oryx is a sad and shameful one, but it may well have a happy ending. Fortunately, this handsome creature is calm and sensible in captivity. It settles down easily to a new regimen and is hardy, reasonably fecund, and quite long-lived. It has, in short, those attributes that make survival in captivity quite possible, even after final destruction in the wild.

Some animals are able to survive in the wild through intelligent and energetic conservation programs. Others are not, either because of habitat destruction that cannot be halted or because of local indifference. Of these latter species, those such as the Arabian oryx that can thrive in captivity will perhaps be returned one day to their old habitat or be established elsewhere. Those that cannot adjust to captivity, and the list is painfully long, will become extinct.

The list of animals that can be seen only in captivity will grow year by year, and any campaign to foster these programs should be encouraged and supported. In this case, what started out to be a story of wanton destruction is proving to be a story of imagination and determination to right a wrong. It is the same human race involved, both as the destroyers and as the savers. It will be interesting to see which force wins.

The Florida Key Deer

NORTH AMERICANS, and especially the citizens of the United States, have seen some of the most tragic wildlife disasters of the century unfold within their boundaries. The bison, the grizzly bear, and the passenger pigeon are but a few examples of a long and sad story.

Shortly after the end of World War II it became apparent that another wildlife catastrophe was about to occur, this time in Florida. That state had already seen the near end of the egret, the decimation of its alligators and crocodiles, and the slow decline of the manatee and had the distinction of being one of the few states in which conservation officers had been not only defied but even murdered.

A survey revealed that the rare little Key deer, a subspecies of the Virginia white-tail and the smallest deer in North America, was about to vanish. It was estimated that no more than twenty-five of these deer, *Odocoileus virginianus clavium*, remained alive on the chain of islands running southwest from Big Pine Key to Boca Chica, seven miles from Key West. They had probably always been confined to the Keys, but the area available to them had evidently contracted rapidly during the war years and their population had decreased drastically.

With a swiftness and determination that could only have been born of bitter experience, a move was launched to save the remnants of the original stock. In 1954, approximately a thousand acres of federally owned land were committed to their salvation by the establishment of the Key Deer National Wildlife Refuge. Surrounding land was put under long-term lease, incorporated into the reserve, and made safe for the endangered animals. The refuge has been built up to include 6,744 acres, covering nearly all of the Key deer's range.

More land is needed, certainly, if the dwarf race is to be properly protected by a buffer zone, but they have responded well. The increase has been tenfold since the alarm was sounded and nearly 250 Key deer are alive today, with a ratio of one buck to three does. In 1963, there were five in zoos.

The factors behind the decline of these little animals are multiple. Land clearing and the resultant loss of habitat were certainly involved, as was continuous killing by hunters. Hurricanes took a toll; fires are known to have been destructive on several occasions; feral dogs have been numerous in some areas where the deer are found. Strangely enough, motor accidents were and are a major cause of death; even now, nine or ten Key deer are struck and killed by cars every year, about a third of the annual loss from all causes. The total loss is in turn about equal to the annual crop of fawns. If motor accidents could be eliminated, the deer would increase rapidly in the years ahead.

It has been suggested that cigarette butts play a part in the accidental deaths. The diminutive creatures apparently find tobacco irresistible and come regularly to the highway to look for butts tossed from passing cars. Like most wild animals (and a tragic number of domestic ones) they have been unable to learn about the automobile. Their small bodies, broken and bloated, are a not unfamiliar sight along the Key West Highway.

The Florida Key deer is a living demonstration that a species (or subspecies) can respond well to sensible conservation measures. Very often it is possible to avert an impending wildlife tragedy if the citizens of a land react swiftly and surely, and in good faith. Surely, although the refuge in the Florida Keys is well patrolled, some natives have poached and shot an occasional deer. Certainly, visitors have carelessly lost dogs or left them behind to form packs and run wild through the tropical vegetation, killing anything available in order to survive. However, a tenfold increase in the deer population in a decade is evidence that most people living or visiting in the area have helped. It is a good sign, and one that bodes well not just for Floridians and other Americans but for all mankind. What one group of people have learned, another can be taught.

Despite the hopeful progress in the management of the Florida Key deer, much is left to be done. The race may only have been given a stay of execution. Six or seven thousand acres are not enough; more land is needed. Something must be done about speeding motorists. If a driver hits a horse, pig, or cow in a free-range state, he can

be sued by the farmer. Should not a nation bring action against anyone who runs down a rare national treasure and leaves it struggling by the roadside?

Are there enough road signs along the highway, warning motorists? Is the highway carefully enough patrolled, not for hunters but for killers with cars? Are there areas where fencing should be added? Are the penalties stiff enough?

Why should there not be some dramatic way of warning all motorists? Two roadblocks would take care of out-of-state travelers who race by in ignorance, and stiff penalties would remind an occasional resident. As for anyone caught running a deer with his hounds or cracking one with his trusty rifle, there must be a punishment to fit the crime.

The stretch of highway that runs through Key deer country is short in a nation rich in superhighways. It would seem that additional protection could be provided to help a herd of rare animals back to strength. If such measures can be taken, the Key deer may yet be saved.

The Mesopotamian Fallow Deer

THE ORDER Artiodactyla contains, in families, genera, species, and actual head count, most of the wild hoofed animals left on our planet. The family Cervidae of this vast and important order contains the true deer, the moose, the elk, the wapiti (in Europe the North American moose is called the elk, and the North American elk is known as the wapiti, its rightful name), the caribou, and the reindeer. There are seventeen genera and approximately fifty-three species. They are all essentially slim, long-legged animals. Antlers are found only on the males of these species, with four notable exceptions: both male and female reindeer and caribou have antlers, while neither sex of the musk deer and Chinese water deer has them (strangely, these two forms have fangs). Antlers, which are shed, are distinct from

11

horns, which are not shed but are appendages of the skull with hard, bony cores.

The Phoenicians knew a beautiful and distinctive fallow deer that ranged throughout wooded lands in areas we know as Iraq, western Iran, Syria and Jordan and from the west coast of the Red Sea all the way to Tunisia. During ancient times the species dropped from sight, not to be rediscovered until 1875, when its existence was again verified. There are two species of fallow deer, *Dama dama* and *Dama mesopotamica*.

The Mesopotamian Fallow Deer

Dama dama is very common, having been introduced by man into widely dispersed areas. Originally occurring along the Mediterranean, throughout southern Europe and Asia Minor, it is now found in Great Britain, in New Zealand, and even in the United States. It is among the deer species most commonly seen in parks and on private estates.

The story of *Dama mesopotamica*, however, the Mesopotamian fallow deer, is a sad one that today causes grave anxiety among conservationists, for there are fewer than fifty specimens left in the wild and the numbers are decreasing, evidently as a result of extensive deforestation and direct destruction by man. These deer are found today along the Karkheh River in the Khuzistan region of southwestern Iran. Here, in an area of less than two hundred square kilometers (124 square miles), the species is dwindling away.

The loss of a major deer species will be tragic. *Takbokka*, as it is known to native peoples, with its peculiar flattened palmate antlers with their numerous points, could easily survive with the help of man. Only the indifference and ignorance of the past have brought the Mesopotamian fallow deer to this extremely perilous point. It need not have been so.

In Kronberg, Germany, there is a small zoo, Georg von Opel–Freigehege für Tierforschung e.V., with a small collection of mammals: 36 species and 123 specimens. Here are found the only two Mesopotamian fallow deer in the world known to be in zoological collections. One of the two was born in the zoo in 1958.

Fallow deer are usually found in relatively small groups in the wild, but in controlled surroundings (and they adapt to domestic environments very well) they become gregarious. This should encourage the establishment of parks in the original range lands of the species above flood level, within forests that have survived, and where fences can be erected to contain small herds that may need emergency feeding from time to time. Sanctuaries are needed along the Ab–i–Diz River in Iran and possibly in areas in the Caspian province of Mazanderan. There are areas in the forested Elburz foothills that are perfect for this purpose, as well.

13

The Mesopotamian Fallow Deer

The Mesopotamian fallow deer is one of the rarest large animals in the world. But, since more than fifty other species of deer still exist, many of them in substantial numbers, it may seem that the plight of this one species is not very important. Fifty-three species, however, is not many. With other endangered species and subspecies lined up to follow the Mesopotamian fallow deer into oblivion (the musk deer, Burmese brow-antlered deer, Manipur brow-antlered deer, Thailand brow-antlered deer, Kashmir stag, several Chinese sika deer, Barbary stag, Bawean deer, Florida Key deer, Père David's deer, black muntjac, Corsican deer, Thorold's deer, Yarkand stag, Bactrian wapiti, Pampas deer, pudu, and several of the reindeer—and that is only a partial list) the Artiodactyla, the even-toed hoofed animals, could soon enough follow the odd-toed Perissodactyla, which, as we shall see in following chapters, are already in a fearfully depleted state.

Nature, we must believe, did not anticipate the destructive potential of her ultimate primate. If the post-Phoenician peoples cut down whole forests without regard for anything but immediate profit, and we are able to put some of those forests back, how do we possibly justify not doing it? If we look at the odd-toed hoofed animals of the world and see the lot of them—a small lot, today—verging on oblivion, and we see the even-toed wild species in too many cases aimed in the same fateful direction, shouldn't we offset this frightening trend by preserving what woefully little we find left to us?

No form of wildlife, no terrestrial form at any rate, is safe today. Even the ubiquitous white-tailed deer of North America, with its myriad subspecies, could soon get into serious trouble without range preservation and careful control of hunting. We *must* preserve what we find. We must establish sanctuaries, we must finance the research and land-acquisition projects of organizations like the World Wildlife Fund, and we must at long last act like the intelligent creatures we presume to be.

Przewalski's Horse

AT ONE TIME the land surface of the earth was populated by vast numbers and almost endless varieties of animals belonging to the mammalian order Perissodactyla, the odd-toed hoofed animals. Today, most are gone; there are nine extinct families that we know of. Only the horses, tapirs, and rhinoceroses remain, and most of these are in trouble or will be shortly.

Among the perissodactyls are the members of the family Equidae, the horse family, with the one genus *Equus*. There are approximately eight species in the genus, including horses, zebras, burros, kiangs, donkeys, onagers, and asses.

The rise of the horse through the ages from the ancient spaniel-sized Eohippus is well known. The form developed through Mesohippus and Protohippus until the genus *Equus* evolved. From the

ranks of these often tacky-looking creatures came fine pure-blooded animals which for man are second in importance only to cattle. Much of his progress in this world was made, or at least made easier, because species of *Equus* were adaptable to life in captivity, hard labor, and highly selective breeding. The handsome mounts we now see in motion pictures and at horse shows are direct descendants of rougher stock that once roamed the earth wild and free.

Today there are probably fewer than fifty true wild horses left roaming free. It is not completely certain that any of these are pure-blooded stock, for they may well be mixed with domestic animals that became feral.

Until 1881 it was generally assumed that the wild horse was gone completely. In that year a Polish nobleman, Count Przewalski, returned from a journey through Mongolia and told of encountering herds of horses that differed from domestic stock, even from the kulans of Mongolia. In 1900, the Duke of Bedford, determined to add a herd of these rare creatures to his game farm, commissioned the famous German animal man Carl Hagenbeck to obtain six specimens. The expedition launched by Hagenbeck eventually returned twenty-eight animals to Europe. These plus two mares and a stallion obtained from a private collection in southern Russia gave rise to a stock that is again spreading itself across the world—this time in captivity. There are at present 121 specimens of *Equus przewalskii* in twenty-nine zoos; all of these are zoo-bred animals.

These 121 animals may be the only pure-blooded wild horses in existence, since authorities suspect that those reportedly remaining free have interbred with domestic animals. Between 1942 and 1945 several questionable specimens were captured in the northern reaches of the Bajjak-Bogdo and Tachin-Chara-Nuru mountain chains. In 1947, and again between 1949 and 1952, six or seven were seen in the Tachin-Chara-Nurus. In 1955 their signs were found in the same area. It is possible that somewhere between 44 and 48 degrees north latitude and 84 and 92 degrees longitude some animals still remain free, drifting with the seasons between China and Mongolia. Most specialists, however, consider the species extinct in the wild.

The decline of the Mongolian wild horse accelerated as Chinese and Mongolian hunters obtained access to efficient firearms. Another factor, undoubtedly, was the increase in herd size of the domestic cattle that came to occupy the same suitable habitat and to use the often scarce water. As is so often the case, the wild could not compete with the domestic stock.

For a long time it was believed that a second species of wild horse, the tarpan, became extinct on the Ukrainian steppes before the middle of the nineteenth century. Many authorities now believe that the tarpan was nothing more than a geographical variety of the Mongolian wild horse, but since the tarpan—with a strange exception—is now gone, the matter may never be settled.

Two brilliant German zoo men, Heinz and Lutz Heck, added to the present controversy over the tarpan when they managed to recreate the animal by seeking out its traits in domestic horses and breeding for these older characteristics. After endless trial and error and many, many disappointments they arrived at an animal that does strongly resemble—if it does not completely duplicate—the tarpan of old. Is such an animal a true member of the species, or is the tarpan, either as a variety or separate species, extinct? It is not an easy question to answer.

The very shy Mongolian or Przewalski wild horse can be distinguished from domestic animals by its erect mane and lack of forelock. It is the size of a rather small domestic horse and has a large head and long tail. It is yellowish on top and almost white on the belly, with its winter pelage lighter than its summer. The herds, which were once evidently very large, seem to have ranged principally on both sides of the Altai Mountains in western Mongolia and in Dzungaria. Some reports, however, seem to place the range farther south in Chinese Turkestan (Sinkiang).

In 1959 the First International Symposium on Przewalski's horse was held in Prague and a program was established to save the species. The Prague Zoo, which has had an excellent record in raising rare equines, now maintains a stud book for all known specimens in the world. Breeding pairs are being established in zoos in a number of countries, and the stock is being built. The present count of 121 is very encouraging for, as befits a true horse, the animal does well in captivity.

Much remains to be done, however. Study programs are needed to determine definitely the status of the species in the wild. After that, Russia should set up a preserve in original range lands and draw upon the domestically raised specimens to rebuild a pure wild herd. Since the horse responds so well to man's manipulations, perhaps generations of men thousands of years hence will still be able to see vast herds of true wild horses racing free with the wind on the barren, open lands of Mongolia, and the brief period when the species was taken into custody for safekeeping by the world's zoological gardens may be forgotten. The horse has been so dramatically important to the history of mankind that we owe future man at least the effort.

The wild and arrogant mustangs of the American West are descended from stock brought to the New World by the Spanish. They in turn—and all other domestic horses—may very well be descended from ancient tarpans and Przewalski horses. It is true that North America once had native wild horses, but that was in prehistoric times, and almost assuredly they were extinct before the invasion of man. At any rate, they are gone now and have no possible connection with the mustangs of today.

Except as domestic animals, and then only in the case of horses and donkeys, the odd-toed hoofed animals have fared poorly since the rise of man. As we shall see, the rhinoceroses are in dire trouble and at least one of the four tapirs is seriously endangered. In the last half century, even the domestic horse has become more of a curiosity than a necessity over much of the world. In the years immediately ahead that trend will continue. We may one day be concerned about the preservation of examples of this man-made animal as well.

It is not enough that the odd-toed hoofed animals should survive as race horses and as handsome draft animals on television commercials. We must put back something of what we have taken away. The project with the Przewalski wild horse of Mongolia seems to be the most hopeful project at the moment. Perhaps we can learn a lesson from the Mongolian wild horse that will be meaningful in ways that are now unknown.

The Cape Mountain Zebra

WHEN THE FIRST white settlers arrived in South Africa, they encountered a wildlife wonderland—and promptly set about the serious business of wiping out as much of it as they could. The success they achieved was singular.

Of the four kinds of zebra that once lived in what is now South Africa, the quagga, *Equus quagga*, has been exterminated. It was a strange-looking creature, a sort of half zebra with only its front quarters striped. The last known specimen died in the Amsterdam Zoo in 1883. Eight years earlier, another specimen died in Berlin. Long before that, all wild specimens had been destroyed on the African continent.

There are two presumed full species of zebra left in southern Africa and one of these has two subspecies: Burchell's zebra, Hart-

mann's mountain zebra, and the Cape mountain zebra. Burchell's zebra, *Equus burchelli,* is hanging on rather well, but some naturalists, at least, question whether it is still a pure strain or has been hybridized. Hartmann's mountain zebra, *Equus zebra hartmannae,* is nowhere common and may face difficulty in the future if care is not taken to maintain the apparently excellent guards that protect South African fauna.

The Cape mountain zebra, *Equus zebra zebra,* is the smallest of the zebras, a close relative of the Hartmann's subspecies and the first zebra known to Europeans. It stands just forty-eight inches at the shoulder and is seldom more than seven feet four inches long. To the Boer-speaking peoples it is *bergkwagga; dauwa* to the Xhosa, *dou* to the Bushmen, and *daou* to the Cape Hottentots. There were eighty-one left in the world at the last available count.

These sure-footed, active little horselike creatures were upland animals. They ranged from Namaqualand through the hills and mountains of Cape Colony to the end of the Drakensberg mountain chain. They have no range as such today. (One of their principal enemies, the Cape lion, is also extinct as a result of the "let's rape a continent" attitude of early settlers.)

It was apparent quite early that the Cape mountain zebra faced an uncertain future. In 1656 the Dutch established laws to protect them, but the restrictions were generally ignored. In 1806, when the British took over the Cape, even this nominal protection was discarded, and the final decline kept pace with the increase in professional hunting. Although they were never very plentiful, they were still fairly common as recently as 1839, but there were only a hundred specimens in 1935, according to the *Journal of the Society for the Preservation of the Fauna of the Empire,* and in 1936, they were further reduced to ninety.

Three Boer families, the Michauses, the Lombards, and the Heinses, managed to save some specimens on their own farms, and to them we owe all credit for the survival of any of the typical subspecies today. In 1937, the Mountain Zebra National Park was established near Cradock, with a breeding nucleus of six animals taken from private farm stock. In May, 1961, there were twenty-three specimens in the park, not a very satisfactory increase in nearly a quarter of a century. In addition to the twenty-three or so in the Mountain Zebra National Park, there are small collections today on farms near Cradock, Outeniqua, and in the Kamanassie Mountains.

The story is a sad one, for there is no reason why this handsome animal should have been treated so badly. It did not interfere with farm interests since when left in peace it spent its time in high and relatively inaccessible places and was in no way damaging.

The extinction of the quagga, the reduction of Hartmann's mountain zebra, and the virtual destruction of the Cape mountain zebra must be laid squarely at the feet of the white settlers. While poaching on the part of native peoples may at one time have given some cause for concern, it is the white man who is guilty. Zebras were killed for their skins, as food for native servants, and as trophies. From time to time specimens were captured and shipped to Mauritius, where the French liked to use them in harness, for which they were totally unsuited. There are reports, although not necessarily reliable ones, that Boer farmers drove whole herds over cliffs for mass kills.

The zebra is an open-land animal that requires no skill at all to hunt. Why has it been hunted, and why is it still being hunted? Hardly a book has appeared in recent years on big-game hunting in Africa, particularly East Africa, without a picture of the "hero" (often "heroine") leaning over the carcass of a zebra, rifle in hand. What is there about this accomplishment that makes men and women want to record it? The animal is not dangerous, does not charge, and in no way challenges the hunter other than by fleeing in panic. Anyone can be driven to within range of a zebra herd by any guide. There are parts of Africa where they can be reached by taxicab!

For whatever reason a man would want to shoot one of these small, peppery "horses" with their incredible striped hides, enough men have done it now to destroy one species, seriously reduce all the others, and to bring the smallest of them all, the Cape mountain zebra, to its present sad plight.

The Cretan Wild Goat or Agrimi

During classical times a wonderful large wild goat with great curving horns was common throughout the Aegean world, in the Caucasus Mountains of Asia Minor, in Persia, and all the way to Baluchistan and Sind. *Capra aegagrus*, the Cretan (or Bezoar) wild goat, also called agrimi, is one of five species in a genus that spread long ago from India to Spain, north into Mongolia and Siberia, and into parts of Egypt, Sudan, Ethiopia, Arabia, and the Greek islands. Like others of its family, this wild goat prefers high, rugged country, the more broken the better.

At present, almost all that remains of this handsome species can be found living a nocturnal life within an area of forty square miles in the Gorge of Samaria at Sphakia and possibly in a few other gorges radiating out from the central massif of Crete's White Mountains. At an altitude of three thousand feet and above, in an area so rugged and inaccessible it is called the "Untrodden," the hundred-odd specimens that are left live on. In recent years twelve specimens were introduced onto St. Theodore's Island and eleven onto All Saints Island. There are claims that a few specimens, possibly interbred with feral goats, have survived on Antimilos, Ghyaros Islands in the Cyclades and one or two islands in the Sporades. There are also thirteen specimens in four zoos, six of which are zoo bred.

It is impossible to estimate the original population of this wide-ranging animal, but it must have been substantial over so large an area. Direct destruction by man is the chief cause of its decline over the centuries; because of the nature of its preferred environment, habitat destruction played a relatively small part in the tragedy.

The history of Crete has been a turbulent one, and the people of this rugged land have been forced to concentrate on their own survival and not on such refinements as wildlife conservation. In 1897, Turkey sent troops onto Crete to quell the endless rioting there, and they brought with them the first modern rifles to reach the island. When the Turks departed they left behind a substantial number of these cartridge-loading rifles, and the fate of the agrimi was sealed. By 1913 they were rare, and the decline has been constant ever since.

The genus *Capra*, of which the agrimi is a species, belongs to the family Bovidae of the order Artiodactyla. This vast family includes, among other animals, the bushbucks, kudus, elands, buffaloes, bison, cattle, antelopes, gazelles, sheep, and goats. *Capra* supplied the first domesticated goats in Asia between eight and nine thousand years ago and is thus a treasured wildlife inheritance. The agrimi has seen all the great civilizations come and, often enough, go. Only modern civilization, though, has come close to achieving the animal's destruction.

It is reported that there are today no more than six men who still climb into the great gorge and hunt goats with rifles and dogs. It would seem that six men could be prevented from extinguishing an entire species, but the people of Crete are not ones to take kindly to outside interference in their affairs, and the laws of the mountain country do not allow for foreigners to come in and tell even six men to stop hunting. Unless enough of these animals can be captured and transferred to areas where conservation laws can have more control, this species will certainly vanish.

Law and order as we know it will not come to the wild interior of Crete in time to save this wild goat. These rugged, individualistic

people have their own rules and they have not yet learned wildlife conservation. It may seem strange that a handful of people can frustrate such a worthy cause, but such is the case, not only in Crete but in many other parts of the world. Until the more sophisticated concept of conservation reaches these diverse peoples, the many species endangered in their various native lands must be removed and held in safekeeping.

The situation in Crete is mirrored in poaching activities around the world. On this ancient island with its turbulent history, rewards have been offered for those who will reveal the names of agrimi hunters. This attempt at preservation has met with little success. Efforts have been made by the Hellenic Society for the Protection of Nature to arouse public interest on the island, but still the agrimi dwindles in number closer and closer to the point of no return. Unless immediate financing is made available to trap and move these animals—and those from the small Aegean islands, where water is in short supply—to protected areas where the herds can be rebuilt, we shall lose yet another species of large animal in our time.

The Giant Sable Antelope

AMONG THE Artiodactyla, or even-toed hoofed animals, there is a genus of special interest, *Hippotragus*. It belongs to the family Bovidae, which is a large and world-wide grouping of highly varied animals. *Hippotragus*, however, is neither large, widespread, nor varied. In fact, there may be only two species: *H. equinus*, the roan antelope, and *H. niger*, the sable antelope, although many experts consider the giant sable antelope of Angola a separate species, *H. variani*, allowing that it is quite similar to the sables of Southern and Eastern Africa but not the same.

The giant sable was first described in 1916 and has been a matter of concern to conservationists ever since. There is good reason to believe that it could easily follow in the footsteps of a now-extinct

member of the genus, the blue antelope or blaauwbok *(Hippotragus leucophaeus)*. By the dawn of the nineteenth century, man had seen to that creature and it was no more.

The glossy giant sable, black, buff, and white (chestnut, buff, and white in the female), with its magnificent sweep of horns, is rated the finest antelope hunting trophy in the world. The male can stand over fifty-five inches tall at the shoulder and weigh as much as 680 pounds, and the handsome face markings make him a Nimrod's dream. He is quickly becoming a conservationist's nightmare.

The giant sable antelope was once found over a broad area in west-central Africa. Today the range is extremely limited, hazardously so. In the war-torn Portuguese colony of Angola there are only two small, isolated reserve areas with a known giant sable antelope population: in the Malange district, a humid area bounded by the Luanda, Cuanza, Dande, and Luasso rivers, some animals are to be found; a little to the north, near Cangandala, in an area of thirty

tropical square miles near the confluence of the Luanda and Cuanza rivers, a few more survive. They are to be seen nowhere else in the world in the wild state.

There has been a recent unexplained withdrawal of the remaining giant sables toward the southern extreme of the reserve areas. The reasons for this are not understood, but with so small a population any change at all is cause for concern. Stability is what is sought, not change, particularly not unexplained change.

Since the area inhabited by these great antelopes is often wild and always primitive, it is difficult to obtain a true estimate of the population. The best-educated guesses put it at 500 to 700 animals, but there could be fewer. The population is far too small, certainly, to allow any relaxation on the part of the conservation-minded. Death for the species could fast overtake the existing stock and push the giant sable antelope over the brink to disaster.

There is an apparent effort to keep the remaining giant sables alive a while longer. Angola has taken some protective measures. The two areas within the range described are officially closed to most hunters, although some licenses are sold. But the political structure of the region is anything but stable. Abrupt change can reasonably be anticipated in the years immediately ahead, and no one knows what this could mean to these rare animals.

The magnificent horns of the giant sable antelope (they can be as much as sixty-four inches long) make a coveted and valuable trophy and fetch a very high price for both native and European poachers. Even today, travelers in the area report no difficulty in obtaining horns, heads, hides, and meat. The official protection of the giant sable, at least to some residents of the area, is only an ironic joke. In plain fact, this animal, that should be totally protected for all time from all forms of hunting and habitat interference, seems to be slaughtered indiscriminately and on virtually a wholesale basis. The man who will buy such a trophy is as bad as the native who traps or shoots the animal to obtain it. The native may be hungry.

Allowing a hunter to kill some of the rarest animals in the world for his own recreation is an anachronism. Today, after seeing a hundred species vanish forever within the last century, after the loss of the passenger pigeon and the great auk, and such animals as the quagga, the plains grizzly, and the several bandicoots, we can no longer permit the privileged hunter to slaughter a species that will never again be seen on earth. Man—who can build a jet plane to fly the hunter to his prey; can freeze dry food so the hunter's diet is rich and varied while afield; can make waterproof clothes, insect-proof tents, comfortable hunting cars, and rifles with superb ballistic performance that make hunting these creatures easier than ever before—must apply his skill and intelligence instead to their sane conservation.

The Javan Rhinoceros

IN EPOCHS long past, the family Rhinocerotidae was spread out in discontinuous ranges from Siberia deep into the heart of the tropics. A dominant mammalian form, the rhinoceroses were represented by over thirty genera. The largest land mammal yet discovered, the titanic baluchitherium, was a member of this widespread and populous family. Massive, ungainly, and magnificently ugly, these great creatures browsed their way across continents and eras.

Most of these genera are now extinct. Today, only four genera containing five living species remain as lingering relics of the Pleistocene age. Every species is approaching extinction. In the genus *Rhinoceros* there are two species, *R. unicornis*, the extremely rare one-horned Indian rhinoceros, and *R. sondaicus*, the Javan or lesser one-horned form, now the rarest large mammal in the world. In the genus *Didermocerus*, there is one species, *D. sumatrensis*, the very rare Sumatran or Asiatic two-horned rhinoceros. In Africa there are two species, each in its own genus: *Diceros bicornis*, the African black rhinoceros (which is not black), is becoming more scarce as the months pass and must be listed as a seriously threatened species; *Ceratotherium simum*, the less aggressive and more sociable square-lipped or white rhinoceros (which is not white), is carefully protected in southern Africa but would soon slip onto the list of extinct animals if precautions were relaxed.

The Javan rhinoceros is the rarest of the five living species, and its story is typical of the rest. This relatively small rhinoceros once ranged through the endless jungle swamps and tall grass and reed areas of Bengal, Sikkim, Assam, Burma, Thailand, Cambodia, and down the Malay Peninsula to Sumatra and Java. The population must have stood in the hundreds of thousands. Today there are about two dozen left on a peninsula at the western end of the island of Java, an area thirteen miles long and seven miles wide at the widest point. This is the Udjung Kulon Game Preserve, established first as a nature monument and then as a full preserve by the Dutch in 1921. The first laws protecting the species were passed in 1909, but until the 93,000-acre reserve was set up the laws were ineffectual. A very few individual animals may be left along the Thailand border, perhaps in the Tenasserim area, and it has been estimated that four or five specimens remain on the Asiatic mainland, but surely there are few, if any, more than that. But even five would be a 20 per cent increase in the world population! In 1945 there were an estimated sixty-six of the species in existence: four in Burma, six in the Malay States, six in Sumatra, twenty-four in Java, eight in Siam, and eighteen in Indo-China. Between 1945 and 1960 fifteen were known to have been killed by poachers on Java alone, and one apparently died there of natural causes. During this same period on the island only two calves were produced, according to the best reports. In late 1960, *The New York Times* carried a feature story about this species, listing the population on Java at thirty-five. Four years later, it was down by eleven.

The Javan Rhinoceros

Rhinoceroses are slow breeders, producing a calf no more often than once every three or four years under the best conditions. With the population so reduced, breeding may have come to a stop even in the reserve. There are no Javan rhinoceroses in zoos today, and none is known ever to have bred in captivity. The poachers may already have won and the species may become extinct in the next two or three decades.

The Javan Rhinoceros

The penalty for poaching on Java was established by the Dutch during colonial days as three months in prison or a fine of 500 rupiahs. Early in 1960 the fine was multiplied by fifteen, but it is still not effective, because a dead rhinoceros is worth so fabulous an amount: Chinese merchants will pay one half the weight of a rhinoceros horn in gold for possession of the treasured item. A small horn may thus be worth 80,000 rupiahs, or more than $2,000. In a bizarre world, a most bizarre fact is that the Chinese, already over-burdened by a horrendous birth rate, use the rhinoceros horn ground into a powder as an aphrodisiac. The hide of the rhinoceros is also big medicine, and one dried hide can bring many thousands of rupiahs. The dried blood is valued too, as is the urine. The market in China alone, of course, is bottomless, endlessly demanding these rare commodities. The supply of rhinoceroses is not as great, and illicit merchants will soon be denied their precious imports.

It is sad, of course, that such profound ignorance and super-stition can bring the end of life forms that come to us from ancient times. The Pleistocene, that weird and wondrous epoch, lives on in these rhinoceros species. Their loss will be tragic.

One cannot stop the demand for dried and pulverized rhinoceros parts in China and elsewhere any more than one can stop the demand for narcotic drugs; the market, a result of fear and ignorance, will almost certainly exist for generations to come. What must be stopped, throughout Asia and Africa, is the poaching of these extremely rare species and the traffic in their parts. The penalties should be made far stiffer, and surveillance should be increased. If these steps are not taken immediately, some of our most important animal treasures will vanish before our eyes. Ignorance will have beaten us.

The Pygmy Hippopotamus

DURING THE Pliocene and Pleistocene epochs the family Hippopotamidae spread itself from Africa and Madagascar to Europe and the
Mediterranean Islands and across Asia to Ceylon. The remains of
many extinct species have been found in numerous and far-flung
deposits. From causes that may never be really understood, the range
of the family contracted down through the centuries more than
climate would seem to have necessitated. There are now only two
genera, each with one living species, and both are restricted to Africa.

By far the better known of the two species is *Hippopotamus
amphibius*, formerly common throughout all of Africa where deep
water could be found. Today, pushed hard by man, the big hippopotamus can be seen only south of 17 degrees north latitude. There

is ample reason for concern in many areas; while not yet a rare animal, it may be heading in that unfortunate direction.

Choeropsis liberiensis, the pygmy hippopotamus, is little known. This stout animal, often no bigger than a large domestic pig, is rare already and its numbers appear to be diminishing alarmingly. It is found in highly restricted areas in the thick primeval forests of the Ivory Coast, Liberia, Sierra Leone, along the River Bia in Ghana and the southeastern corner of Guinea.

Although the two hippopotamuses are each other's closest living relatives, they are distinctly different in appearance and habit. The pygmy is darker and about one third as long, one half as tall, and one twentieth the weight of the great hippopotamus. (A great hippopotamus is approximately twelve feet long, almost five feet tall, and weighs about four tons; a pygmy is five to six feet long, two and a half to three feet tall, and weighs about five hundred pounds.) The pygmy has a rounder head with eyes on the sides and not protruding above and its snout is more modestly proportioned. The pygmy is not nearly as social in habit, is generally nocturnal, and is not aquatic in the same way that the larger animal is. Although the pygmy is always found near water and in forests where hidden streams are common, it spends relatively little time submerged. If startled on land, the great hippopotamus heads for the nearest water very much like a submergible express train. If startled even very close to water, the pygmy will inevitably turn away and crash inland through the thick growth on the forest floor.

The status of the pygmy hippopotamus is inadequately known. It was afforded complete protection (Class A) by the London Convention for the Protection of African Fauna and Flora in 1933. No one can judge how many of these animals are left in the pockets of their wild and remote habitats. Some reports seem to indicate that the population in very restricted areas is rather dense. On the other hand, travelers have spent years in their known range without seeing a single specimen. This is certainly not only because of the scarcity of the animals but also because they are nocturnal, shy, and resident in some of the thickest forests and swamps in the world.

With so remote a range and with such elusive habits, one would think the animal would be in little danger. However, the pygmy is not adaptable to new wild habitats, is not a rapid breeder, and will always give way to the industries of man. While the range of man is expanding, that of the pygmy hippopotamus is contracting. Serious ecological studies are badly needed lest we wake up one morning and find only one species of the family Hippopotamidae left.

Although probably not hunted assiduously, the pygmy has flesh favored by native populations, who are, for the most part, desperate for protein in their diet. It reputedly tastes like wild pig *(Sus)*. One behavioral characteristic of the pygmy works invariably to its disadvantage: it is a creature of habit and uses regular trails through the thick vegetation. In time these routes form tunnels, and the animal falls easily to snares set for it by hungry natives. No one can say how many fall this way every year, but the number may be dangerously high for the species.

On the other hand, the human natives of the area are so poorly nourished that any realistic conservation effort must integrate human needs with the total conservation plan. Conservation, like all other sciences, must work in concert, not in limbo. We cannot hope to save the remaining wildlife of the world by our love for animals alone; we must be guided by love for sorely deprived peoples as well.

Strangely, for an animal so shy in the wild, the pygmy hippopotamus breeds regularly in captivity. There are today over eighty specimens in zoos, thirty-five of which were born there. The Basel Zoo alone has raised twenty-eight specimens, and other zoos have fine records as well.

The rather unattractive pygmy hippopotamus may seem remote and unimportant in its dense jungle home. It is, though, a rare survivor from another kind of world. It is descended from strange and great primeval mammals long gone from our planet. Along with the larger and more widely distributed big hippopotamus, this last of a mighty line of ponderous creatures is of scientific interest and is a rare natural treasure that should be protected.

Baird's Tapir

THE MAMMALIAN FAMILY Tapiridae must have once been spread across vast areas where it is no longer known. This is suggested by its present discontinuous range. In the one living genus there are four extant species. *Tapirus terrestris*, the Brazilian tapir, is found in South America only. The wooly Andean or mountain tapir, *Tapirus roulini*, is similarly restricted. Far off in Asia a third species, the Asiatic tapir, *Tapirus indicus*, is found in Burma and Thailand, on the Indo-Chinese peninsula, and in the Malay States and Sumatra. Baird's tapir, *Tapirus bairdi*, is presently found in Ecuador and Colombia west of the Andes (where it overlaps ranges with the Brazilian tapir), from the Gulf of Guayaquil in the south to the Sinú River in the north. It is found as well in isolated areas up through Central America to Mexico. It is most common in Mexico in the wet forests of the southeast, extending north to southern Veracruz and west to Oaxaca.

The former distribution of this particular species is not known, although certainly its populations were much denser throughout its present range. Baird's tapir is the only member of the order Perissodactyla native to North America that has survived into recent times. The perissodactyl wild horses or mustangs of the western part of the United States are feral, as we have seen, descended from steeds imported from Europe by the Spaniards. This tapir is the lonely remnant of a once-splendid mammalian fauna. It can give us only the slightest hint of what a zoological wonderland the broad North American continent once must have been.

Known to science only since 1865, the shy and retiring Baird's tapir is already very rare and is believed to be decreasing in numbers. As its loss would represent the end of an entire mammalian order in the vast land mass of North America, this decrease is giving conservationists cause for considerable anxiety.

The tapir, Baird's tapir specifically, has been exterminated over much of its range. Today, it is found only in the wildest and least disturbed forests. It evidently requires the proximity of rivers, lakes, or swamps as well as deep forests, climax forests being most favored. It adjusts poorly and retreats whenever man and his dogs appear. Although agile on land as well as in the water, it does not seem to be able to survive once its habitat is disturbed. Forest clearing, agriculture, and road cutting spell doom for this donkey-sized animal.

Resident in North America since the Oligocene epoch and almost certainly once found as far north as Alaska, Baird's tapir no longer has a secure population anywhere. Living alone or in pairs, it is slowly slipping away from us. In the dense, wet jungles of southern Mexico and down through the nations of Central America, solitary animals are hiding as far from mankind as they can get. Theirs is a sad and lonely lot, for the highways and industrial pursuits of man are slowly carving away and slicing up their range. Isolated pockets die out as breeding becomes more and more difficult. Without large primeval areas through which they can move, tapirs are seriously threatened.

Baird's Tapir

Crowded into restricted habitats, they fall victim to the jungle cats which relish their flesh. The jaguar is the tapir's worst enemy, aside from man, but the mountain lion, the tayra, and the smaller cats all prey on the young at least. The mother tapir keeps her single young with her for a year, but she cannot effectively protect it from stealthy feline hunters. Driven together into ever smaller areas, cats and tapirs are poor companions.

Although Baird's tapir is permanently protected from hunters in Mexico, immediate and decisive action is needed to assure freedom from encroachment and range destruction. There are virgin rain forests left in Mexico that could be set aside for the perpetuation of this unique species. An area on the slopes of Volcan San Martín in the Tuxtla range of southern Veracruz and others in southern Campeche, Quintana Roo, and Chiapas should be maintained as a permanent, inviolate rain-forest national park. Baird's tapir, and other indigenous species now endangered, might then survive.

Fortunately, Baird's tapir does quite well in captivity. There are presently eleven in six zoos, and two of these are zoo-bred specimens. An animal reduced to the verge of extinction by range destruction cannot, however, be preserved temporarily in captivity and then returned to its natural habitat unless its natural habitat is also preserved. If parts of the natural range cannot be saved, the only member surviving in North America of a great and varied mammalian order will be forever dispossessed.

The Orangutan

At the top of the primate ladder and therefore at the top of the pyramid of animal life (except for man) is the family Pongidae. The five living genera and approximately ten species include chimpanzees, gorillas, gibbons, and the sole species of genus *Pongo*, the orangutan (from Malay *orang utan*, "man of the forest"), *P. pygmaeus*.

At one time, orangutans or their close relatives were probably widespread on the Asiatic mainland as far as India, and possibly from Peking to the Celebes. But that was long before firearms. Today, the species is found only in parts of Indonesian Sumatra (where it is known as *mawas*) and in small, confined pockets on Borneo. On Borneo (where the native name is *mias*) the orang is found scattered in small areas in Sarawak and Sabah and in western

Indonesian Borneo; there are none in Brunei. Nowhere is there protection effective enough to meet the problems that are forcing the species into a position where extinction seems almost certain.

In recent years there appeared to be a fairly substantial population in North Borneo southward to the Sembakong area of northeastern Indonesian Borneo. However, in 1965 battle erupted between Indonesian expansionists and Malaysian interests along the border in North Borneo. British artillery operating in behalf of Malaysian interests raised havoc with the shy apes. Small bands were already suffering terribly from the assault of new farmers and logging crews; the new death toll had a devastating effect on the already dwindling population, and the disruption was probably even more damaging.

The orangutan population began to decrease before World War II, and there has been a severe reduction since that time. There seem to be between 2,000 and 5,000 of these reddish-haired, four-foot-two-inch tall primates left in the world, with most estimates favoring the lower figure. Orangutans breed slowly and have a long 210-to-270-day gestation period. A female does not produce her single young more often than once every four years, and infant mortality is estimated at 40 per cent. For these reasons, despite a long life, a female may not produce more than two or three young in her lifetime that will in turn survive to breed.

Little is known of the orangutan in its native habitat. Until very recently, no comprehensive studies of wild populations were attempted and more nonsense than accurate information was available. The sociable, peaceful, gentle, even lethargic ape has generally preferred lowland swamps and, despite stories to the contrary, has never been a problem for man. Although immensely powerful (the armspread can be more than seven and a half feet) the ape is not known to attack man except in extremely rare cases, and then only in self-defense. The number slaughtered in years past, ostensibly because the species was dangerous to man, were killed by pleasure hunters or misinformed settlers.

Nearly the only area of Sumatra left where the orang survives is the state of Atjeh, an area of intense European economic develop-

ment in recent years. Habitat destruction is widespread and devastating to the species. Much potential habitat has recently been found empty of specimens and the implications are tragic. The species, which has been rolling back before the assault of man for decades, now seems to be collapsing.

Recently, meeting my wife at a pet shop in a large American city, I found her sitting with a three-year-old orangutan in her lap. The great red-haired baby was sucking on my wife's thumb and making wonderfully engaging cooing sounds. The dealer offered us the specimen for $3,500. Only the fact that their size at maturity and their lack of understanding of their own strength make them totally unsuitable as pets kept us from rushing to the bank to arrange the unusual purchase.

The probable history of that little orangutan has haunted us since that day. No doubt a native in Malaysian Borneo, hunting in his own territory or south into unprotective and indifferent Indonesian Borneo, fired an ancient gun loaded with scrap iron at the infant's mother as she frantically sought cover in the thick trees of a jungle swamp. As she fell dead or dying to the ground the native scooped the baby up and melted into the undergrowth. Somewhere in a village or along a river the native sold his prize for about $5 to a "wholesaler," who in turn sold the baby in Singapore for about $290. The purchaser obtained forged certificates, saying that the specimen had been captured legitimately on a license in Indonesian Borneo; the price would then go to about $1,600 for infant and papers. By the time such a specimen reaches the United States or Europe, the price is about $3,500. The greater tragedy is that a producing female was needlessly destroyed to obtain the baby, and other females in the troop may have lost their infants in the hysterical scramble to avoid the hunters. In addition, for every living example of this vanishing species to reach the west, six to eight others die en route.

Author Barbara Harrison recently studied eleven baby orangutans that had been rescued from Dyaks, who had killed the mothers to capture the infants. Typically, a new arrival was about a year old, grossly underweight, suffering from lack of milk (orangutans nurse for two years or more); they were often worm-infested and infected with malaria, one or more skin diseases, chest colds, or pneumonia, and suffering from injuries as well. One female about a year old weighed less than six pounds and had a broken arm. A male suffered from worms and pneumonia and weighed only six pounds, although it had full deciduous dentition. Three of the eleven died, despite careful and heartfelt veterinary care. This cruel picture is typical.

The illicit traffic in infant specimens has caused the serious decline in the species as much as anything else. Ostensibly working to supply European and American zoos and circuses, these traffickers in animal agony have operated unhindered for years. Their callous treatment of these extremely sensitive and intelligent animals is a shocking condemnation of a supposedly enlightened society of men.

Since the traffic has been so heavy and so long-running, it is not surprising that there are approximately 280 specimens in zoos today. Thirty-seven of these were born in captivity, although the survival rate of infants in zoos is low. (The Rotterdam zoo bred seven specimens but was able to raise only five.) With ninety-six zoos today recording orangutans in their collections, one wonders how many acquired specimens from really legal sources, how many mothers were shot, and how many other infants died to make these exhibits possible.

Immediate action should be taken on a number of fronts if the orangutan, one of the world's truly great apes, is to survive for the wonderment and awe of future generations of man. The illicit traffic must be halted. This is best done if the western countries make the import of specimens illegal. No self-respecting zoo will knowingly break the law to exhibit a bootlegged animal. The International Union of Directors of Zoological Gardens has agreed to exclude all illegally collected orangutans. Singapore should ban the import and export of specimens under any pretext. If there is no legal way of moving an animal in or out of the port, forged papers will be of little use. Sabah in northern Borneo must have a permanent sanctuary immediately, and its confines must be guarded.

The Orangutan

The Bako National Park in Sarawak should be studied carefully and further developed to make a reserve in which to re-establish orphaned animals. Punishment of natives and Europeans alike caught killing or disturbing the surviving troops should be severe. Small fines are a mockery and many natives look upon a short jail term as a well-fed vacation. Europeans are less fond of jail in the tropics, however, and natives do not like long-term hard labor.

There are probably fewer than ten species of apes left. The orangutan is on the verge of extinction and the gorilla, as we will be seeing, is in serious trouble. There will never be any more apes than there are now; the species that survive our stupidity and cruelty will exist in the future. The ones that fall before us will never rise again.

The Mountain Gorilla

Known to science only since 1847, the mountain gorilla, giant ape of the eternally damp forests of West Africa, has inspired more nonsense than sense among the uninformed; there are many misleading accounts of its strength and ferocity. Until very recently, even scientists were ill-equipped to supply accurate information to offset popular misconceptions. The mountain gorilla has consistently been one of the least known and most poorly understood of the large and important land animals left on our planet.

The classification of the gorilla, also, has been confused for many years, and taxonomic battles have raged. In 1929, H. J. Coolidge set forth an encouragingly simple classification when he revised the genus *Gorilla* to include two subspecies: *G. gorilla gorilla* of West

Africa (Nigeria, Gabon, etc.), the lowland gorilla, and *G. gorilla beringei* of Central Africa, the mountain gorilla. Specifically, this latter population can be found in parts of eastern Congo, as well as in isolated areas in southwestern Uganda and western Ruanda. The total area encompassed probably includes no more than 35,000 square miles. Less than 25 per cent of this area has any gorilla population, however. Few, if any, of these animals range north of the equator or farther south than 4 degrees 20 minutes, a north-to-south range of just about 300 miles. The total east-to-west range is no more than 220 miles. That is a small portion of a planet as large as the earth, a part we should be able to spare or at least share peacefully with the greatest of the great apes.

There are certainly fewer than fifteen thousand mountain gorillas left today, conceivably fewer than ten thousand, and possibly fewer than even five thousand. Gorillas do not readily sit still for a census, and even a man as thoroughly knowledgeable as George B. Schaller could be no more specific than to estimate that the population stood between five thousand and fifteen thousand in 1963. Whatever the exact count, it is far too small for safety. There are probably no more than twenty specimens in zoos today and, unlike the lowland gorilla, none have been bred to date. Zoos will almost surely be successful in breeding and raising mountain gorillas in captivity once the immature specimens now available mature, but their slow rate of reproduction would make it impossible for zoological collections to re-establish or add to wild populations. The mountain gorilla will never respond like the bison. Once the population begins a serious decrease, extinction will result.

Female gorillas probably are capable of reproducing any time after six or seven years, but males do not achieve sexual maturity until they are nearly ten. Gestation takes about as long as for humans, but the mortality rate is very high. Scarcely more than half the gorillas born in an area reach six years of age. Fewer yet live to breed. A female may let four years or more pass between offspring; this fact, coupled with the mortality rate and an initially small population, does not bode well for the future.

Although an area 650 miles wide separates the short-haired lowland gorilla and the long-haired mountain gorilla, the two animals are so much alike it seems certain they were once part of a continuous population. Natural forces and not the intrusion of man probably caused the rift. Gorillas are fussy about both their habitat and their food. Changes are not welcome; troops would be quick to withdraw, for example, from any area suddenly affected by an increase or decrease in rainfall.

Gorillas inhabit only humid forest areas where succulent herbs and tender vines are easily found. They do not enter open grassy areas for more than a few minutes at a time and will not cross large bodies of water. It seems reasonably certain that they cannot swim; they seldom even wade. Any animal that can be stopped by a river or stream, by an open field, or by a dry area is bound to find it difficult or impossible to branch out and establish new and independent populations. Although there were surely more gorillas during the Pleistocene epoch, there were probably never very many. Even if the population then was many times as large as today's, the gorilla would always have been relatively scarce.

When compared with other animals discussed in this book, the gorilla might seem to be relatively safe. Even a minimum estimate of three thousand specimens is better than thirty, forty, or fifty individuals. Still, the area these animals inhabit is small, and incursions upon their territory and directly upon their numbers are relentless. It would take little to push the mountain gorilla too far, with extinction the result.

In areas with good agricultural potential, the range boundaries of the mountain gorilla are constantly being pushed inward. Habitat destruction is equally constant. The hunting of gorillas by natives for food is extensive and damaging. Zoo collectors have been known to take a fearful toll by shooting helpless adults in order to obtain infants with a minimum of trouble. The mortality rate among these immature captives as a result of simple ignorance and callousness can be enormously high. Few of these infants reach their destinations alive or in a condition to survive; it is doubtful that more than

one in ten captive gorillas will be alive a year after being taken. This great loss is made sadder and more reprehensible by the widespread slaughter of adults in the process of the initial capture.

There is still more pressure put on the mountain gorilla population by the demand of certain laboratories for specimens, and there are still men who consider it sport to shoot a gorilla with a high-powered rifle. Since the gorilla is inoffensive and seldom attacks a man other than to make false rushes and a lot of noise in their famous ceremony of intimidation, the "sport" is somewhat difficult to comprehend, and the man who will slay a gorilla today for enter-tainment will be as much an enigma to men a century from now as the emperors of Rome and their matinee blood baths are to us.

Six dormant volcanoes sit astride the border between the Repub-lic of the Congo and Ruanda. Known as the Virunga volcanoes, their damp and forested slopes have long been the home of numerous small groups of mountain gorillas. As many as four to five hundred animals may yet survive on those slopes. In 1925, Albert National Park was established by the ruling Belgians solely for the protection of these animals. In 1929 the park was enlarged. Since 1960, the independent Congolese have controlled the park and have apparently been hearteningly conscientious in their efforts to maintain the sanc-tuary. Intrusion by cattle-owning tribesmen from Ruanda has been frequent, however, and heavy damage to the foliage has resulted in some areas. Left unchecked, these "banks" of useless cattle (they are maintained for prestige, not for food) would soon denude the valuable slopes. The mountain gorillas in the area would be doomed.

In 1930, five years after the establishment of Albert National Park, the British Crown set aside the northern slopes of three of the Virunga volcanoes in Uganda as a gorilla preserve. Twenty years later, private interests gained control of four of the original thirteen square miles and the best gorilla country in Uganda was taken from the species. Human traffic is quite heavy in the remaining nine miles of this preserve, and the gorilla population is not permanent.

The adjoining land belongs to Ruanda, and that government, which in 1958 relinquished nearly eighteen thousand acres of reserve forest land to farmers, has shown little interest in cooperating. The gorillas in this area may already be doomed by an irreversible course of events.

The Kayonza Forest in Uganda seems to be in a good state, although the gorilla population is almost certainly small, under two hundred specimens from all evidence. Since the isolated population in the forest seems to have reached the area through a now-lost forest bridge from the Virunga volcanoes only fifteen miles away, it probably has not long been independent. Out on a limb as they are, the few animals left in the area could very quickly be affected by any incursion, and the situation requires constant monitoring.

The relatively little forest land left near and on Mount Tshiaberimu in the Congo is threatened by human incursion. Unless immediate steps are taken, the small isolated bands northeast of Lubero may be wiped out in the near future; there are probably fewer than fifty animals left in the area.

There are three areas in Kivu province, Republic of the Congo, where the gorilla population seems safe for the moment. In the wet lowland areas near Mwenga, Fizi, and Utu, human endeavors do not seriously conflict with gorilla habitat requirements. Although the picture is momentarily bright, no situation in Africa is permanent.

In discussing conservation it can be difficult to explain why a specific animal should be saved. To point to some remote or little-known creature of small size and no economic importance and plead its cause can seem fruitless. The mountain gorilla, though, is an animal even the unknowing can care about. It is great in size, richly wrapped in legend, humanoid yet magnificently primeval. It is awesome to see in the zoo and a great attraction when displayed on a circus poster. Yet, preyed upon by tribesmen, politicians, farmers, husbandrymen, and hunters, the mountain gorilla stands poised on the brink of total destruction.

The Aye-Aye

IN 1780, an unusual animal was added to the roster of strange creatures from Madagascar. The extraordinary aye-aye, *Daubentonia madagascariensis*, rarest of the lemurlike animals, was found in the eastern and northwestern portions of the island.

Today, the aye-aye is nearly gone. A few seem to live on in small enclaves within the range reported at the time of their discovery and identification. There are none in zoos, as far as is known, and none are known to have bred in captivity, although they have been shown in zoological collections from time to time in the past.

The only surviving species of the family Daubentoniidae, the aye-aye is as delicate as it is rare. It can survive and reproduce, apparently, only in the forests, mangroves, and bamboo stands of

Madagascar. Although virtually nothing is known of its breeding habits, it seems that the animal has a low reproduction rate. It is believed that one young is born annually to a pair. A larger species, *Daubentonia robusta*, was known from the Pleistocene epoch but is now extinct. It almost certainly lasted until recent times, because its teeth were used in native ornamentation, and it is highly unlikely that the teeth were obtained from fossil sources.

The nocturnal and generally solitary aye-aye is not a lovely creature. Its head is short and round and there are patches of bristles above its eyes, on its nose, cheeks, and chin. Its eyes are large and round, its ears large, rounded, naked, and black. Its tail is bushy and accounts for one half of the aye-aye's total length of thirty-six inches. It feeds on the pith of bamboo, sugar cane, beetles, and insect larvae. The only people who appear to love it are the Betsimisaraka natives, who believe that aye-ayes house the souls of ancestors. Love is more like fear, in this case, but the result is a happy one: the natives leave the aye-ayes alone.

The reasons for the decline of the aye-aye are not clearly understood. Destruction of habitat has contributed but other causes remain unknown. At any rate, a reserve is urgently needed to protect whatever stock remains alive. The forest of D'Ambato Malamo in the Feherive district of Tamatave province would seem to be a desirable location. If the aye-aye lives on, it is probably here.

Why become exercised over the fate of a primitive little primate on the remote island of Madagascar? The aye-aye has never been a popular pet; it has seldom been seen in zoos, probably never in circuses; they are probably poor food, and their fur is worthless.

There are many reasons to preserve this small animal. The aye-aye is a living creature, subject to human morality and respect for life. The aye-aye is rare, the only surviving member of a family. It is a primate, albeit a primitive one, and interesting to science for that reason. It represents a whole group of animals that arose and remained isolated on a single island and are worth studying in this regard.

The Aye-Aye

There are only eleven surviving families of primates and a number of these are in trouble. Soon only some tenaciously raucous monkeys may remind us of the great and fascinating group from which man evolved. No one could hold that the aye-aye is our direct ancestral form, but the creature is undeniably kin. If this is not sufficient reason for protecting the aye-aye, surely it would be hard to find better reasons for destroying him.

The Red Wolf

The wolf has been maligned throughout history as few other animals have. Endless superstition, astounding quasi-religion, boundless hysteria, and a highly questionable "science" have operated together to urge the animal's extinction as quickly as it could be accomplished. Every man's hand has been turned against the wolf, legendary and real, and only the remarkable tenacity and intelligence of the animal have enabled it to survive at all.

The wolf has fared badly in North America, particularly in the United States. Today, the gray or timber wolf has vanished from almost all of the states except Alaska, although it has survived in Canada. In the lower Mississippi Valley, the red wolf of the southern woodlands has met even more difficulty. Unable to retreat to the Canadian woodlands, the red wolf has reached the very brink of extinction, and the death of only a few specimens will push it over the edge.

The red wolf, *Canis niger,* subject to an amazing amount of taxonomic conversation, is a species apart from the better-known gray wolf. The area of its range probably never equaled that of the larger gray wolf and it achieved the status of a species over some opposition.

In Louisiana, Arkansas, Oklahoma, Texas, Missouri, Kansas, Illinois, Indiana, Kentucky, Tennessee, Georgia, and Florida the red wolf once ranged, often overlapping with the gray and possibly occasionally interbreeding with it. As land was settled and domestic stock brought in, the wolf was forced back. Overgrazing by cattle upset the natural plant balance; flash floods, erosion, and drought further reduced the wolf range. Timbering destroyed much of the woodland to which small packs had retreated, and endless hunting, trapping, and poisoning increased the death toll. Unhappily, killing a wolf is still considered a proof of manliness in some areas.

With its natural prey under constant pressure, with a gun waiting for it every time it showed its head, the red wolf decreased in numbers steadily from the mid-1800's on. Officially excused as predator control, unwarranted destruction was directed against the species. Legends of man-eating beasts, the superstitious dread of werewolves, and similar anachronisms seemed to justify the slaughter, and even many early conservationists were quiet.

In 1932 there were a few small packs in western Mississippi, perhaps a dozen animals in sixty square miles. They are now gone. In 1940, fifty-nine specimens were captured in Missouri, and the population from which they came is probably completely destroyed by now. The Ozark Mountains in Arkansas may still provide cover for a few, and isolated areas in eastern and northern Louisiana still support a small population. The number of red wolves surviving today is not known, for the area involved is vast and in parts well wooded, but that number cannot be high.

Reports of red wolves and complaints of their attacking livestock can better be attributed in most cases to feral dogs. Also, the

coyote has been extending its range, and perhaps some blame can be laid there. Whatever the actual cause of the reported attacks, the red wolf is not strong enough in any area of the United States to justify continued slaughter.

In Arkansas and Louisiana, the wolf is listed as an unprotected species that can be killed at any time by any means. How can the species survive? The red wolf has been reduced to probably a handful of specimens without any significant action being taken to preserve it. No one will even know when it finally vanishes, and few, it seems, will care.

There are six specimens of the red wolf in three zoos today, and some hope may be seen in the fact that three of the six were born in captivity. Wolves that are well cared for and not abused settle down in captivity quite well and breed once they have established themselves. If not crowded together too closely, females will raise their young with the same incredible care and attention they give their offspring in the wild. Perhaps, before it is too late, enough specimens may be placed in captivity—where traps, guns, and poison cannot reach them—there to reproduce as living examples of yet another species driven from the land.

The Spectacled Bear

IN THE ORDER Carnivora there is a particularly fascinating family of animals, Ursidae, the bears. The family includes the two largest remaining terrestrial carnivores, the Alaskan brown bear (specifically those on Kodiak Island) and the polar bear. It also includes animals that have been at war with mankind since before the dawn of history, when the contest between the caveman and the short-faced cave bear must have been horrendous.

The bears have not fared well. They tend to be of a rather unpredictable temperament, and there have been unfortunate cases of attacks on man. These attacks cannot accurately be called unprovoked, though, since man is forever harassing the bears he encounters. In any specific attack, the victim may not have been provocative, but the bear had probably been provoked almost every other time it had encountered man in the past.

In addition to the slaughter engendered by the belief that they are dangerous to man, bears are "big game" and every hunter's gun is turned against them for that reason. Also, as feeders on carrion, bears from time to time work over carcasses of domestic animals dead from other causes, only occasionally raiding stock themselves, and have earned an undeserved reputation as inveterate stock killers. They are hated by farmers and ranchers and are listed as unprotected vermin in most parts of the world.

There are always special problems with large carnivores near human habitations, and bears have attracted particular attention because of their large size and obvious habits. The occasional mauling of a picnicker has not helped.

In the last half of the eighteenth century the Atlas bear vanished from Morocco, leaving no bears in any part of the great African continent. In North America, the Mendocino grizzly was gone by 1875, Henshaws grizzly by 1895, the California coast grizzly by 1908, and the Klamath grizzly by 1911. The Tejon and Southern California grizzly both were exterminated by 1916. At least nine other subspecies (or, perhaps, geographical varieties) of grizzly bear, including the great plains grizzly, have vanished in the last hundred and fifty years. The black bear has been driven into ever smaller pockets over its once vast range; the Mexican grizzly is at present giving cause for concern; and, as the next chapter shows, the polar bear has recently been found to be in danger.

In all the vast land area of Central and South America there is only one kind of bear, the only species in its genus, *Tremarctos ornatus*, the spectacled bear. This medium-sized bear formerly ranged through enormous areas in the mountainous regions of western Venezuela, Colombia, Ecuador, Peru, and western Bolivia. Throughout all of this area this animal is now apparently exceedingly rare.

Although primarily a forest animal found to an altitude of ten thousand feet, the spectacled bear does wander out into higher clearings and onto lowland savannahs. It may be more of a vegetarian than most other bears, although it does eat meat when it can get it. Its lowland forays have brought it into contact with man and his ever-improving rifles. The results may already have been disastrous.

The status of the spectacled bear is inadequately known. A survey is needed to determine how bad things really are and to decide what steps must be taken to prevent the extinction of the only bear in the southern half of the western hemisphere.

Not very long ago virtually all of South America was a vast wonderland of wildlife, a magnificent and seemingly unending sanctuary. The coastal strips were settled by Europeans, and inland there were tiny cultivated islands, largely remaining from colonial days. These settlements hardly affected the over-all wildlife picture. The continent was so vast and the human population so small in comparison that it seemed the wildlife could never be threatened.

But revolutions come, not just political revolutions but great changes that affect whole populations and whole continents. South America is undergoing just such a revolution now. The Iberian-Indian stock is emerging from almost unspeakable poverty, and the land-raiding that has occurred on every other continent is taking place. Industrial and agricultural development is causing the destruction of wild habitats and virgin forests at an alarming rate. At present, there is no other comparable land area whose people are less conscious of conservation than South America. Even Africa is alert to its problems compared with this continent.

When man extends his range over the land, the great predators are often the first to suffer. South America is no exception. Wealthy hunters from other lands are discovering that the wildlife of South America offers them exciting challenges, and they are invading virgin areas in increasing numbers each year. None of the countries involved has effective wildlife protection facilities. Hunters are tourists, and tourists mean revenue.

As hydroelectric projects, highway building, mining, industry, agriculture, and logging activities increase in the years ahead, some of the world's most exciting wildlife treasures will be lost.

The Spectacled Bear

No one would seriously suggest that South America go forward in the poverty of the past in the name of conservation. However, wildlife areas should be set aside before it is too late. Surely, the lessons learned in Europe, North America, and most recently in Africa can be applied to find the means for integrating national progress with fauna preservation. Although there are some extraordinarily sincere conservationists in South America working toward this goal, they are still too few and without power to make their demands heard in the council chambers where the future is being planned.

The jaguar, the puma, and the spectacled bear, as the largest carnivores on the continent, are going to suffer the most in the years immediately ahead. The two cats will be able to survive longer just because they are cats. The bears will roll back before the industrial avalanche, and their extinction is almost assured within the next hundred years unless provisions are specifically made for their preservation.

There are forty-six spectacled bears in twenty-six zoos today, thirteen of them zoo-bred specimens. This is encouraging, because it shows these animals can do well even in a completely controlled environment. But it is not enough. Preserves should be sought out and established with purpose and determination. The emerging nations of South America should avoid the tragic mistakes made in the rest of the world. The seemingly unending wildlife resources of North America did not last forever; perhaps part of those of South America can still be saved.

The Polar Bear

Listen to the words of Herb and Miriam Hilscher (*Alaska, USA,* 1959):

> Kotzebue and Point Barrow are crowded in the Spring with big game hunters who seek to bag the vanishing polar bear. . . . At the present rate . . . polar bears will soon be attractions . . . found only in zoos.

Clyde Ormond, hunter and hunting expert, wrote (*Bear!*, 1961):

> The popularity of polar bear hunting has catapulted . . . to fever pitch.

Speaking of some guides and outfitters but, in all fairness, not of all, he added:

> They set the hunter down in the general proximity of the bear, then, with . . . low flying . . . herd . . . the beast . . . to within rifle range.

The Boone and Crockett Club, whose founding father was Theodore Roosevelt, is the arbiter and record keeper of North American big-game hunting. Some measure of the increasing interest in polar bear hunting can be found in their latest record book, published in 1964. Of the twenty-five largest polar bears known to the records of big-game hunters, fourteen have been killed since 1960. A trophy bear is rated in total points achieved by adding the length of the skull (minus the lower jaw) to the width of the skull at the widest point. The world record bear was killed in 1963 and rated $29^{15}\!/_{16}$ points. The second largest, rating $28^{12}\!/_{16}$ points, was killed in 1958.

It once was something of an accomplishment to hunt and kill a polar bear. Even if one is not in sympathy with hunting at all, it must be admitted that traveling by sailing ship and then by dogsled to slay one of these monsters (they are the second largest meat-eating land animal in the world) with a rifle of questionable ballistic performance was a man-sized task. More than one hunter perished in the attempt.

Today, things are somewhat different. A hunter can leave New York City by jet and arrive in Anchorage about twelve hours later. The round-trip ticket costs about $500. After another plane ride to Kotzebue, the hunter meets his guide in the hotel lobby. Drinks and talk about hunting follow, and the party leaves as soon as the weather clears. Two planes are used, in case one gets into trouble.

The guide asks about $2,000 per hunter for a ten-day trip. Many guides "guarantee" a bear; no bear, no fee. There are, certainly, hazards to be met but they usually involve plane crashes and not the actual encounter with the quarry. The results of the ease and safety of hunting polar bears are beginning to tell.

The range of the polar bear has been contracting for centuries, but the decrease has been especially marked since the 1930's. This great white predator, *Thalarctos maritimus*, was known in ancient times on the shores of Japan and Manchuria, as well as in Iceland, where it hasn't been seen for nearly a century. Whalers, sealers, and fur hunters pushed the bear back into the far northern latitudes. Intensive hunting began in the early seventeenth century, and by the early nineteenth century the polar bear was endangered in most parts of its range. Only recently was this really appreciated. Even today most people think of the polar bear as having always lived "at the North Pole" and nowhere else. Actually, the North Pole is too far north for even a polar bear.

Now found only in the higher latitudes—Greenland, Canada, Alaska, Svalbard Islands, the archipelagos north of the Russian coast, Franz Josef Land, Novaya Zemlya, Severnaya Zemlya, New Siberian Islands, Wrangel Island—the polar bear may number ten thousand specimens. Alaska, Canada, and Norway seem to have the most substantial concentrations; Canada alone may have six to seven thousand of the ten thousand suggested for the whole world. The annual kill by hunters world-wide may be in excess of 1,300. The once-large Greenland and Soviet Union populations have been sadly depleted by hunting.

Polar bears are not rapid breeders. In the wild, a female may give birth to one or two cubs every third year. It takes a long time to replace a 28- or 29-point white bear skull!

With new transportation facilities, with radar, with transarctic crossings by submarines, with regular transpolar flights by commercial aircraft, with portable nuclear power plants, the Arctic is no longer the remote place it once was. New military requirements make the once-remote and forbidding Arctic a place for new sciences and exploration. Cities are going to be built in the far north, and it will become in time a matter-of-fact recreation area. All of the animals of that vast region—whales, walruses, seals, musk oxen, caribou, reindeer, wolves, wolverines, the fantastic array of bird life, the foxes, and the polar bears—all must suffer. If we do not launch immediate programs of study and conservation, we will make of the newly opened Arctic a greater wasteland than ever it was before.

The polar bear is not without protection even today. Canada allows only Indians, Eskimos, and a small group of license holders to hunt the species. Greenland and Norway restrict and govern hunting reasonably well. The Soviet Union outlawed hunting the polar bear in 1956. There are closed seasons in Alaska.

This inconsistent legal protection is not enough, however. Polar bears migrate over large areas and may fall under more than one set of regulations in the course of their travels. Since they are circumpolar, their protection is an international problem; in fact, there is a definite need for an internationally coordinated program of study and conservation of all Arctic fauna.

The polar bear is one of the most commonly exhibited bears in the zoos of the world. One estimate puts more than a thousand of them behind bars and moats. They are good breeders in captivity, and most zoos of any consequence breed their own specimens. With some zoos it is an annual event.

Man's attitudes toward the polar bear are contradictory. On the one hand we have the grave concern of conservationists and the recent rating of the beast as rare by the International Union for Conservation of Nature and Natural Resources (IUCN). On the other hand, sporting magazines carry numerous advertisements of lodges and hunting guides asking you to come hunt polar bear with them. As Bob Wallack says in his *U. S. Hunting Atlas* (Maco Magazine Corporation, 1965): "The hunter has a warm, cozy bunk in a Point Barrow hotel and gets airborne when the weather permits." Times have changed. The polar bear may not be able to.

The Cheetah

THE CHEETAH, *Acinonyx jubatus*, with its approximately ten sub-species, once ranged widely throughout the arid and semiarid regions of India west to Egypt, Libya, Morocco, Rio de Oro, and throughout Nigeria, Sudan, Somaliland, and south to the southernmost part of the African continent. Except in the forested and particularly moist areas, cheetahs were common over most of this vast land mass. There may have been a second species, sometimes referred to as *Acinonyx rex*, the "king cheetah." In the middle 1920's, specimens were taken in east-central Rhodesia that had black stripes as well as spots. We may never know whether these were the remnants of another species or just a few aberrant individuals.

The hunting leopard, which the cheetah is often called although it is distinctly not a leopard, must have been very common through-

76

out much of India. The Mogul emperor Akbar (A.D. 1556–1605) is said to have maintained over a thousand captive specimens for use in the hunt. From ancient times until quite recently the innately docile cheetah was the plaything of the wealthy. Because cheetahs tame easily, they were kept as pets and used to course game in a manner not unlike that of hounds today, although only a single animal was used.

The destruction of the cheetah's natural prey, the smaller hoofed animals, probably was a principal cause for its decline, although direct destruction played a large part as well. Also, this is a shy animal and for reasons not clearly understood does not thrive in a habitat with heavy human traffic.

Although the cheetah is timid, it has been killed by hunters throughout its range. In 1947 a "sportsman" killed three specimens in India in one night, using artificial light. They may have been India's last three cheetahs, since the 1952 spotting of a lone animal in Madras (Chittoor district) has never been verified. In fact, the cheetah is probably extinct throughout Asia except for Iran and Russian Turkestan where a small number apparently survive.

In the arid and semiarid areas of South, East, and North Africa, the cheetah is hanging on by a thread. The species appears to be approaching extinction subspecies by subspecies. The form from South Africa has all but disappeared from Cape province. It survives in small numbers in some areas, but there are virtually none in Orange Free State, Natal, or the Southern Transvaal. Except in South Africa's parks, where there are fewer than a hundred, they will vanish completely in the years immediately ahead.

In East Africa it is approaching extinction in Kenya. It is still hunted by some men, and its natural prey is vanishing so rapidly that it will not long survive unless special measures are taken. Although certainly the fastest four-footed animal alive, the cheetah is not as good a hunter as might be presumed. Because it runs too fast to maneuver, it often misses prey that dodges, and without a large number of prey animals to choose from, the cheetah can soon get into serious trouble.

The Sudan cheetah persists in extremely restricted areas, but the stability of the population is doubtful. The Senegal cheetah is extremely rare; it is found on some remote semiarid plateaus but is now rare in Tunisia as well as in Egypt. Until very recently it had been afforded little protection, and the protection it is now getting in some areas may have come too late.

The cheetah is not known to have attacked man. When chased on horseback, it does not turn and face its tormentor. Even when captured as an adult, it soon settles down to peaceful coexistence with humans and quickly accepts them if they show no hostility. I once intercepted a full-grown male cheetah in flight on East 67th Street in New York City. It had been badly frightened outside of a television studio by a boy firing a cap pistol at it. We rolled over together in the gutter, and when it raised its paw as if to strike

I offered the same gesture. Its anger quickly subsided without issue. There can be no more docile large cat than this!

Some farmers have lamented that cheetahs attack farm stock, and they have hunted them for this reason. As the animal's natural prey diminished, the cheetah must have taken to raiding pasturelands occasionally, but by this time the cheetah was surely so far reduced in numbers that damage to financial interests could not have been great enough to warrant the assault the species has had directed against it.

There are about 187 cheetahs in eighty-four zoos today. None of these are zoo-bred specimens for, although there are records of cheetah matings, the infant mortality is extremely high. There are reasons to believe that this is true in the wild as well as in captivity and the high mortality could contribute to the animal's decline.

The Cheetah

Lions are apparently strangely intolerant of the cheetah, perhaps because they hunt much the same prey, often in the same area. As wild areas diminish, this hostility may increase. Although a cheetah can outdistance a lion easily in open pursuit, once it is caught or ambushed the cheetah has little change against the larger cat.

Prey destruction, animal husbandry, and direct destruction by man do not seem to account for all of the species decline in recent years; the decrease has been too sudden. Perhaps an unknown contributing factor such as disease is responsible. Certainly further studies are badly needed.

The cheetah is scientifically interesting because it is the only cat without retractable claws. It represents in its own way the world as it once was. Its movements, its very appearance, are aesthetically stimulating. However, man has wanted this animal dead more than he has wanted it alive, and the cheetah has responded in the only way it could, by vanishing. There is a very real danger that the cheetah—inoffensive and beautiful, elegant and swift—will disappear from Africa just as it has from India and most of Asia.

The Spanish Lynx

AT ONE TIME most of Europe was the natural home of a handsome, self-sufficient cat of relatively small size and large spirit. Related to similar animals in North America and northern Asia, the European lynx *(Lynx lynx)* weighs anywhere from fifteen to fifty pounds, depending on subspecies and individual variations.

In ancient times the lynx was hunted for its fur, and that practice stopped only when there were virtually no more lynxes to hunt. As agriculture and animal husbandry spread and began to demand more and more space, deforestation caused a rapid decline in the lynx population all over Europe. Unfortunately, some lynxes liked domestic pigs, chickens, ducks, geese, colts, calves, lambs, and kids as much as they liked more natural prey, and man turned his hand against these cats with particular fervor. Without forest land to

which it could retreat, lynxes began to disappear. Wardens killed them on sight to protect game animals for the privileged hunter, and the last forest strongholds were denied the species.

Today, the European lynx has been exterminated in the British Isles, France, Denmark, Switzerland, Italy, Austria, and Hungary. It is all but gone in Germany, Poland, Yugoslavia, Bulgaria, Rumania, and Lithuania. The breeding stock in both Sweden and Norway may soon be endangered. In most areas the lynx is listed as vermin, and there is no closed season. Control of this cat is justified but surely total destruction is not.

Recently, the Dutch National Appeal of the World Wildlife Fund raised enough money to launch an ecological study to determine ways of re-establishing the species in protected areas. It is hoped that this study will eventually be extended to cover all of Europe and give the European lynx a second chance. Many subspecies, of course, are gone beyond recall.

At one time a subspecies, *Lynx lynx pardina*, the Spanish lynx, ranged over nearly all of the rugged Iberian peninsula. Only the fact that Spain still has some wild and sparsely settled areas has enabled this subspecies to survive. In total, there are probably several hundred left today. The present range includes the Toledo Mountains, Sierra Morena, the lower Guadalquivir River, and some areas of Estremadura. The northern limit is the Peña de Francia. Some specimens almost certainly remain well hidden in the Pyrenees.

The Spanish lynx must be considered very rare today. It has been much reduced during the last half century and appears to be decreasing in numbers at the present time. The causes for the decline in Spain are the same as in other parts of Europe: direct destruction, ostensibly to protect domestic stock, and extensive deforestation.

The largest Spanish lynx population remaining, between 150 and 200 specimens, is to be found on the Coto Doñana in the delta of the Guadalquivir. The area includes one of Europe's most important marshlands bounded by some of the continent's highest sand dunes. Here migrating waterfowl by the uncounted thousands spend a part of each year; here also are six known eyries of the Spanish imperial eagle, of which there are probably no more than 150 specimens left in the world. Here, the lynx can be at home.

Recently, $574,610 was raised from private donations, a substantial bank loan, and a grant from the Spanish government for the purchase of twenty-five square miles that could be held permanently as a great marshland preserve. Projects underway or planned for the draining of the Coto Doñana Marismas make this preserve of tremendous importance not only to Spain and the people of the Iberian peninsula but to all of Europe. Although partially protected throughout the Coto Doñana area, between fifteen and twenty lynxes are shot each year under special license. No one knows how many are shot by poachers.

There are eighty-five European lynxes in thirty-five zoos today, fifteen of which are zoo-bred specimens. Only ten of the eighty-five are Spanish lynxes, and they can be found in just three zoos.

As we have seen problems arise whenever large predatory animals are forced to live near human habitations. When farms are involved, inevitable stock losses lead to a massive counter attack, with the animal almost always losing. Farming has always been a difficult life, and there is precious little mercy for any creature that makes it harder.

Hopefully, we are more enlightened today than when the lynx was driven from most of Europe and will work to save a wonderful species of animal, even though it is a predator. The fact that over half a million dollars has been spent in Spain to save a "swamp" would appear to be a sign that this is so. Perhaps this is the turning point, and Europeans will now start back up the long, hard road of rebuilding their precious fauna. There are still a few wisents in zoos, still deer in private collections and in parklands, still some Spanish imperial eagles and Spanish lynxes on the Coto Doñana. Something can be done. Europe will be richer by far when men can once again move through forest lands and hear the sounds of the natural world. Many fine symphonies have been composed in Europe over the centuries, but none finer than this. The music of the natural world is not a reflection of man's soul but a part of it.

The Asiatic Lion

THE GENUS *Panthera* of the family Felidae (order Carnivora) includes some of the most handsome and exciting animals in the world. To this genus belong the jaguars, the leopards, the tigers, and the lions. These animals, symbolic of wildlife in general, are among nature's most powerful predators.

Most people think of the lion as an African animal, although the heraldic symbol of India is the Asiatic lion, *Panthera leo persica*. Actually, the lion has probably been in India longer than its close relative, the tiger. The subspecies that has managed to hang on in India once ranged widely through Asia Minor, into southern Europe, in Palestine, Arabia, all the way through Iran, Iraq, and south in India to the Narbada River. They were gone from Greece by about

A.D. 100, from Syria not much after that, and from Palestine by the end of the Crusades.

There are persistent reports of lions surviving now in Iran and Iraq. The Kharkheh River Valley and Bakhtiari Mountains in Iran are scrub covered, sparsely populated, remote, and extremely wild. There was a sighting there in 1941. It is doubtful that there are any lions left now, but if a few should exist they would be found in these two adjacent areas. There are similar reports from Saudi Arabia, but it is unlikely that even the oases on the Upper Euphrates support any lions today.

The Bible mentions the Asiatic lion more than 130 times, giving some indication of the large number there once must have been. There were dense populations throughout the central, western, and northwestern parts of India at least. A well known story tells how a "sportsman" by the name of Colonel G. A. Smith shot nearly three hundred specimens during the mid-1800's. Another hunter killed

eighty in just three years, shooting from horseback. By 1884, the lion was gone from all of India except the Kathiawar Peninsula in the western Indian state of Gujarat. There, on the southwest portion of the peninsula, in an area called the Gir Forest, the Asiatic lion survives.

The Gir Forest is a semiarid area with a great deal of thorn scrub and patches of stunted timber, including a quantity of undersized teak. It is not a forest in the real sense of the word and is a favorable habitat for the lion, which feeds on nilgais, sambars, chitals, and the much-favored wild pigs. The Gir Forest covers some 480-odd miles, and here about 290 lions can still be found.

There has been a great deal of speculation as to why the tiger has survived so well in many parts of India—as has the leopard— while the lion has fallen back before spreading civilization and blossoming agricultural pursuits. There appears to be no justification for the romantic notion that the tiger drove the lion to the edge of extinction, because the lion and the tiger occupy different ecological niches. The tiger is a jungle cat, or at least a cat of thick reeds and heavy grasses. It is found in moist areas. The leopard, too, is a cat that seeks the cover of dense growth. The Asiatic lion, like the African, is an open plains animal and avoids thick vegetation. Also, in the days when conflict might have taken place, there was plenty of hoofed game to go around. The two great cats were more apt to avoid each other than fight.

The tiger survived where the lion could not because the tiger is a more cunning animal, more secretive, more nocturnally inclined, and more difficult to hunt. This is also true of the leopard.

The lion was killed off for two reasons. As with many other animals, it was killed, first, as a potentially dangerous predator. As humanity spread throughout India in ever-denser concentrations, the lion was easily destroyed once firearms were generally available. The second major factor is what some people think of as sport. Military personnel stationed in India with leisure and unlimited firepower at their disposal made a major contribution to the virtual destruction of this species. The lion was also victimized by native princes. In the state of Saurashtra in India, within which the Gir Forest lies, there were once 202 princes each with his own small empire. Since the lion was listed in the area as "royal game," it is not difficult to imagine the havoc raised by princely hunts mounted to entertain visitors. It is hard to see how the lion reached the twentieth century in India at all.

There are major problems in the Gir Forest today. Although the lion has been protected there for decades, it is not a game sanctuary and at the present rate could become unsuitable for the lion in another two decades. With its fewer than five hundred square miles, the area is home to seven thousand people as well, and about sixty thousand domestic animals. Professional graziers and villagers drive herds of goats, cattle, sheep, and buffaloes into the area, and the food supply for local hoofed wildlife is dwindling rapidly. It takes many hoofed animals to maintain a lion population, and the lion will take domestic stock when natural prey is driven off or destroyed. The decline in natural prey forces the lion more and more to hunt domestic stock, with the inevitable retribution. It has been suggested that one hundred lions a year are poisoned by disgruntled villagers because of stock losses. That figure seems a bit high, considering the total population of under three hundred, but certainly there are dangerously high losses. Increased animal husbandry and the failure to declare the area a national park or inviolate game sanctuary will mean that the lions will have to be established elsewhere or vanish in the foreseeable future.

There have been efforts to establish the Asiatic lion in other parts of India. None gave much hope of success until 1957 when three specimens were released into the Chandraprabha Sanctuary (the poetic name means "radiance of the moon") in the northern Indian state of Uttar Pradesh. This sanctuary is only forty-three miles from Varanasi (Benares) but the small stock is increasing. Fortunately the lion shows great biological potential and produces healthy cubs regularly. The first cub was killed by poachers in June of 1958, and another cub died of unknown causes. It is hoped, however, that the small group has caught hold. The area resembles African lion country and may be the answer to the Asiatic lion's survival.

There are thirty specimens of this subspecies in nine zoos at the present time, and, quite encouragingly, eighteen of these were born in captivity. Like their close African relatives, the lions of Asia reproduce readily behind bars and moats.

Although on superficial examination the Asiatic lion does not differ profoundly from the African subspecies, it is an animal apart. It was a great predator over a vast area that is no longer capable of supporting such an animal. In India, though, where it has resided since extremely ancient times, it has shown remarkable tenacity, clinging to life against a mad barrage of gunfire and despite the boredom and callousness of Indian royalty and British military alike. The lion belongs in India, it is a part of the land, a part of the history, and a good part of the natural splendor of the nation. It would be shameful if a few hundred square miles in the vast subcontinent could not be set aside and made safe before it is too late. Soon enough the lion in Africa will face the same problems. Perhaps we can learn in India and transfer the lesson to Africa.

The Caspian or Persian Tiger

THE TIGER, commonly thought of as a jungle animal lurking in lands laboring under the burden of eternal heat, is still common in India and can be found in many areas in humid southern China, on the Malay Peninsula, in Sumatra, Java, and even in Bali. That is not where the story began, however, for the tiger is almost surely an animal of the far north. It may have appeared first in eastern Siberia near or above the Arctic Circle. In what could have been a two-pronged migration, it expanded southward and, to an extent, westward. The animal never reached Borneo or Ceylon, but much of the rest of Asia knew the steady tread of this great cat at one time or other. Though it is very closely related to the lion (anatomically they are almost indistinguishable), the tiger never got to Africa.

The stories of all the tiger subspecies are sad ones. The Manchurian or Siberian tiger *(Panthera tigris longipilis)* is nearing the end of the line; it is estimated that there are fewer than a hundred left in the world. The Korean tiger *(Panthera tigris coreensis)* is similarly reduced to the point where recovery would seem to be impossible. The Chinese Turkestan tiger *(Panthera tigris lecoqi)* is probably already extinct. The Javan tiger *(Panthera tigris sondaica)* has a very limited range and is reportedly below ten living specimens in strength. The lovely Bali tiger *(Panthera tigris balica)* probably survives in fewer than five living animals. The Caspian or Persian tiger *(Panthera tigris virgata)* will serve as a detailed example of the rest.

The great ten-foot-eight-inch Caspian tiger has a range listed as Transcaucasia, Iran to north Afghanistan, to the Aral Sea, and Lake Balkhash in Russian Turkestan. The range was formerly much more extensive, and even the distribution now given is unrealistic. The last tiger killed in the Transcaucasus was in 1932, although a few may since have come back to the region from Iran. They occasionally enter Turkmen from that area. No one can know, of course, the exact remaining number of so elusive an animal moving through so vast an area, but it is safe to estimate that it is totally extinct over most of its range, with perhaps twenty cats left in Iran and possibly another few dozen in Russian Turkestan. A decade or two ago the few animals that appeared briefly in other parts of the former range were apparently migrants.

The World Wildlife Fund places the Caspian tiger in Category 1: "Very rare and believed to be decreasing in number." They append a notation: "Giving cause for *very grave anxiety*." The italics are theirs.

There is no doubt about the causes behind the decline of this magnificent animal. There are several factors, of course, but most can be put under the heading of direct destruction by man. There has been some habitat destruction, to be sure. In central Asia the burning of thickets along watercourses has caused the decline of the tigers in Kazakhstan to the point where they are probably gone

completely. Thousands of acres of magnificent Caspian forest were destroyed, and the tiger lost yet another home.

There has been destruction of prey, too, in most areas. The tiger requires a great deal of animal flesh to feed its own four hundred pounds or more. It has suffered and failed to breed as a result of the loss of prey and has been forced to wander out into areas where the guns of man could be turned upon it. The control of malaria in many areas once inhabited by the Caspian tiger has also resulted in increased human activity inimical to this great hunter.

Man is the major cause of decline. Wherever the tiger goes, wherever it shows its great head, a gun or trap is waiting. The tiger is killed for sport, to avenge crimes it probably never committed, for its magnificent hide, and because it is a predator.

Is there really any hope for the Caspian tiger? Probably not. It is too big, too handsome to survive. The ritualistic overtones to tiger hunting are not to be resisted. Manhood can be bought that way, and hunters are not to be denied manhood.

The zoos of the world house many rare cats. The tigers do quite well in captivity, although they do not breed nearly as readily as lions. During the first half of the 1960's many rare tigers survived in zoos. There have been ninety-six Manchurian tigers, forty-four Sumatran, four Javan, six Amoy, and even eight Korean, but sadly no Caspian. It is extremely doubtful that there ever will be again.

The really great cats of the world will eventually all follow the Caspian tiger on the long, desperate road to species annihilation. If man would only leave some of the world intact, he could live with all creatures great and small, but by senseless destruction of habitat, by slaughter of natural prey, he time and again drives the land's original predators into direct conflict with his own economic interests and then destroys the predators, destroying as he does so all chances for the land to regain a natural ecological balance. Man the destroyer is having his day.

The Black-Footed Ferret

Among the many interesting branches of the Carnivora is the family Mustelidae, the weasels. About fifteen species of the genus *Mustela* are spread across North and South America, Europe, Asia, Java, Sumatra, Borneo, and northern Africa. Included are the true weasels and such animals as the ermine, mink, ferrets, and stoats.

One of the most interesting members of the genus is the elegant, black-masked, black-footed ferret, *Mustela nigripes*. This largely nocturnal creature was not described until 1849, when Audubon obtained a skin and made extensive notes on the apparently new species. It was many years before this animal was universally accepted into the scientific fold. It is the only North American counterpart of the old world black-bellied weasels, the polecats of eastern and northern Asia.

The Black-Footed Ferret

The black-footed ferret once ranged on the interior plains of the Rocky Mountain foothills from the western Dakotas to northern Montana and Alberta, southward to Texas and into central New Mexico. Found to altitudes of 10,500 feet, it always appeared in the vicinity of prairie dog towns, apparently requiring abandoned prairie dog burrows for shelter and living almost exclusively on the flesh of these sassy, communal rodent relatives of the marmots. This dependence has caused the black-footed ferret to become one of the rarest mammals in North America and possibly the rarest mustelid in the world.

The decline of this handsome weasel species can be attributed without hesitation to the direct destruction of the prairie dog through extensive poisoning campaigns. At one time throughout the states included in the original range, there were incredibly large prairie dog towns. Some towns would extend for ten or twenty miles or more and contain millions of animals. The black-footed ferret, moving through such a wonderful living larder, led a good life indeed. Even in those days, men at the edges of these vast rodent communities

could seldom see a ferret. Nature adapted the animal to be able to appear in form like the prairie dog, although it is of a decidedly different shape. When it sits up and folds its distinctive black feet against its chest, it is quite indistinguishable from the creatures around it except to the well-trained eye.

Farmers and ranchers, somewhat understandably, found these huge concentrations of rodents incompatible with agricultural interests. A great deal of potentially valuable crop and grazing land had been prairie dog country. But man went overboard. There was little attempt, until most of the damage was done, to establish a pattern that would enable the prairie dog, and therefore the burrowing owl and the ferret, to survive. Destruction was indiscriminate and in many areas complete. Today, prairie dog towns outside of national parks and monuments are extremely rare.

As a result, the population of the black-footed ferret is not only precariously low but it is apparently declining. This is cause for grave anxiety, for there seems to be relatively little that can be done to offset the unfortunate trend in most areas. Between 1946 and 1953,

about seventy specimens were seen in forty-two different locations. One third of these specimens were dead. In addition to deaths from loss of prey, automobiles may kill as much as 10 per cent of the ferret population every year.

The black-footed ferret has just one chance for survival: conservation forces must continue the Fish and Wildlife Service policy of trapping them wherever they are found and transporting them to national parks and wildlife sanctuaries where they can re-establish themselves and maintain their unique species.

Certain areas, particularly, offer promise. Wind Cave National Park in South Dakota was established in 1903. It contains forty-four square miles and still has a substantial prairie dog town. Since hunting and poisoning are forbidden within its boundaries, the black-footed ferret could survive. There are other good areas in Texas, Oklahoma, and South Dakota under the control of conservation forces that would seem to suit the needs of the species as well. Theodore Roosevelt National Memorial Park has also been suggested as a likely habitat to receive transplants.

Since there are only five specimens in two zoos today and there are no records of recent zoo births, what is done for the black-footed ferret will have to be done in natural surroundings.

From time to time young of this species show up in New York and other large cities for sale by the larger and more sophisticated animal dealers. With a total population that has probably not exceeded one hundred in decades, this traffic should be stopped and all available specimens made wards of the federal government.

The great prairies of North America were once one of the greatest of all wildlife wonderlands, ancient or modern. Life rolled across these vast, open lands in numbers and variety that defy the descriptive powers of any writer. Most of that is gone, directly destroyed by man. The bison survives because a few men dared run against the current and fight for its preservation. The unique pronghorn has survived for the same reason. The prairie chicken, as we shall be seeing, is not doing as well, and many of the predatory birds are in serious trouble, along with the prairie dog, black-footed ferret, and many other species. The plains wolf and plains grizzly did not make it at all.

To denude further these vast lands of species is to throw away a part of America's history and a part of her heritage. It is also to muzzle the protest Americans wish to make about what is happening in Africa and in many other parts of the world. Americans should spend more time, more money, and more thought on preserving natural prairie lands and the species that are historically a part of those lands. To fail to do this is to relinquish the rights of Americans to be heard in the conservation council chambers of the world.

The Sea Otter

IN RECOUNTING the tragedy of the world's wildlife, we can occasionally tell a story with a happy ending. Such stories are "good for the soul" and stand as proof that conservation efforts do pay off and that man is capable of making great advances toward rebuilding something of the natural world despite the terrible destruction that has gone before.

In 1741, a Russian expedition of exploration led by the Danish navigator Vitus Bering was shipwrecked on one of the Commander Islands. Bering died, but some of his men survived on a barren wasteland of an island. During their ordeal they managed to kill eight hundred animals they called *bobrof*, referring to them as beavers. In fact, these men were the first Europeans to know the great sea otter, *Enhydra lutris*, the only species in its genus. The

Russian sailors found the otters satisfactory eating and also noticed the superb quality of the animal's pelt. They saved the pelts and, when they managed to build a boat and sail back to Siberia the following summer, they carried the skins with them.

The sea otter is three times the size of the fresh-water river otter, growing to a length of four and a half feet, and has the most valuable fur in the world. The Russians were not long in recognizing this. Expeditions were mounted, and, in the years immediately following, the Russian Empire was extended along three thousand miles of North America. The slaughter had begun.

The animal the Russian hunters pursued ranged from Lower California up the coast to Alaska and the Aleutian Islands, among the Kuriles and the Commander Islands, and along the coast of the Kamchatka Peninsula in Asiatic waters. Sea otters must have existed in vast numbers, for they eventually supported nearly 170 years of fur trading.

In 1867 the United States purchased Alaska from the Russians, and the rate of slaughter increased. By 1900, the animal was rare. Ships that might once have brought back five thousand pelts were lucky to return with two dozen. By 1910, it was generally believed that the sea otter was extinct, although Alaska was thought to have a small breeding stock left.

Not knowing whether they were protecting an animal or a memory, the United States, Great Britain, Russia, and Japan signed a treaty in 1911 making the hunting of the sea otter illegal. It was a somewhat belated gesture, and for over two decades it appeared that it had been in vain. Then, early in the 1930's rumors began to circulate that the sea otter still existed. In 1938, ninety-four specimens were discovered off Monterey, California. In 1936, a thriving colony was discovered in the waters off Amchitka Island.

By 1957 the Monterey colony had increased to approximately 500 animals. There are probably 40,000 sea otters alive today, and they are on the increase.

A federal law prohibits even the owning of a sea otter pelt without a special permit. The animal is strictly protected and care-

fully supervised by constant study programs. Although it has rebuilt its colonies off central California, western Alaska, and in the Commander and Kuril Islands in the slightly more than half century of its protection, it still has reoccupied only one fifth of its former range.

The capturing of sea otters is forbidden, so there are none in zoos today. From 1955 to 1961 a single female lived in the Woodland Park Zoo, Seattle, the only one known to have been successfully maintained in captivity. There have been, of course, no zoo breedings.

There is no doubt that the sea otter will continue to extend its range, avoiding shipping lanes, industrial and sewage discharge, and areas frequented by too many small-boat enthusiasts. One day it

should again be a common animal along thousands of miles of coastline. And some day, someone is bound to point out that there are
hundreds of thousands of sea otters in shallow coastal waters, bear-
ing the most precious fur in the world, a fur that by decree was once
worn only by royalty in some Asiatic countries. It will be pointed
out that a small fortune could be reaped with little effort each year
without "seriously reducing the sea otter population." Some con-
gressmen and senators will agree with this point of view. Abalone
fishermen working along the California coastline have already com-
plained that the sea otters are eating them out of business, since
these large mustelids include a few red abalone in a diet made up
mostly of sea urchins and mussels. There will be mounting pressure

to resume the slaughter. What will we do? Will we allow it to start all over again, or will we leave the world's most valuable fur on the animal nature intended to wear it?

There was once an approximate counterpart of the sea otter off the coast of the northeastern United States and the Maritime Provinces of Canada, known as the sea mink. It is believed to have been twice the size of its land cousin and was probably once reasonably abundant. Its former existence was not even known until after the turn of the twentieth century, when a few bones were discovered in an Indian kitchen midden in Brooklin, Maine. Today, all we know of the extinct sea mink has been learned from a few bones and two pelts in very poor condition that survived. As we have seen, the sea otter, on the other side of the continent, nearly disappeared also and could still face extinction if trading in this fur begins again.

At the time protection was belatedly extended to the sea otter, there were probably only a few hundred left alive, whose existence was not even known. Yet for once man did act. The result constitutes one of the happiest chapters in the whole history of conservation and must stand as a monumental example of what can be done. We have on earth today nearly a thousand other opportunities to prove that we do care. How many of these opportunities will we seize?

The Giant Panda

THE GIANT PANDA is the symbol of the World Wildlife Fund, and although it cannot be listed for certain as a seriously endangered animal, it is rare—and restricted to a perilously small habitat range. Most of all, it is tremendously appealing and is therefore a logical choice for an organization whose great works are dependent on public sympathy, support, and cooperation.

It is not easy to put *Ailuropoda melanoleuca* into a pigeonhole. It is not a bear, of course, and it is not a raccoon either, although puzzled zoologists have placed it in the family Procyonidae, which also contains the raccoons. Sharing the family with the raccoons and the giant panda are the various ring-tailed cats (which are *not* cats), the coatimundis, the kinkajous, and the strange and gentle little Himalayan red panda. The red panda is much closer to the raccoon than to the giant panda. There are eighteen species in the family, in eight or nine genera, depending on your choice of authority. Sometime during the Miocene epoch, the true dog family developed splinter groups evolving the ancestral raccoons and the early bears. The giant panda somehow seems to fit in between the two. One cannot help feeling that we have a lot to learn about its actual relationship to other animals.

Virtually nothing is known about the former range of the giant panda, although fossil finds of a closely related animal suggest that it may once have been found on the Upper Yangtse in Szechwan province and perhaps in Burma. That, however, is highly speculative. Here again one must feel that there is much to learn.

Today, the giant panda may be restricted to the highlands of the central and western parts of Szechwan province of southern China. It is found in the Tsing Ling Mountains and, according to some reports, in eastern Tibet and even in northern Yunnan. There are many conflicting opinions as to where this elusive creature may live today. The areas involved are extremely remote, often virtually inaccessible, little traveled in the past by reliable witnesses, and peopled largely by rather primitive tribes. The panda seems to spend most of its time somewhere between six and eleven thousand feet above sea level. Most reports suggest that it seldom leaves these altitudes and is unknown in the lowlands. Other reports are conflicting.

The panda is solitary except during the breeding season and is most difficult to find, hence the dearth of information. If approached, despite its considerable size, it will seem to dissolve into the thick bamboo forest or into a cave or rock jumble. It will also take to trees if pursued, although it is essentially a ground dweller.

The giant panda is said to live exclusively on bamboo shoots or roots, but specimens have been observed eating several kinds of tufted grasses, gentians, irises, crocuses, and, as if to substantiate the placement of the family among the Carnivora, fish, rodents, and small birds. It appears, though, that bamboo is the favorite food.

The giant panda has been something of an enigma since its discovery in 1869 by Père David, who was pursuing tales of a white

bear in southern China. No one knew then and no one knows now the size of the population. The animal may be very rare or quite plentiful. The consensus would seem to be that the species is safe for the moment but requires careful watching.

At one time the great interest shown in the giant panda by visiting zoologists and animal trappers was misinterpreted by local natives, and the species was hunted rather assiduously. It soon became apparent, though, that the skin had very little commercial value, and the senseless hunting eased off. Today pandas are apparently little bothered. China has strict laws protecting them, and there is reportedly considerable local pride in the species. It has become known even to people on the tribal level that this animal is something very special and should not be pursued. Since the habitat and diet of the giant panda keep it from conflicting with human interests, it may continue to live its present quiet existence for some time.

The giant panda always has been rare in zoos, although it is inevitably a favorite wherever it is exhibited. At the present time there are two in Canton, a single female in London, a male in Moscow, three specimens in Peking, and three in Shanghai: ten specimens in all, in five zoos. The entire zoo world was delighted to learn in 1963 that the pair in the Peking Zoo had successfully bred, producing a female cub. It was the first known zoo breeding of this strange animal species.

Because it is safe, at least for the moment, the giant panda is an example for all to observe. It is the kind of animal that could be quickly destroyed. If gold or some other precious metal were discovered in its mountainous home, one shudders to think what would happen. Let us watch the giant panda, both for its protection and as a reminder of what wonderful things can happen when an animal is allowed to carry on in its own ancient ways without the profound disturbance of continuous human encounters.

The Tasmanian Wolf or Thylacine

AUSTRALIA, when it was opened up by European settlers, offered one of the most remarkable collections of animals to be found on the planet. Here, in isolation and relative peace, the ancient marsupial animals, those mammals lacking the placenta and generally possessing a pouch, branched out into most of the ecological strata. Parallel development with more advanced placental animals in other parts of the world could be seen in case after case. In this vast, often uninhabited land a magnificent zoological "laboratory" had developed.

Although there is evidence that a series of climatic and environmental changes adversely affected the Australian fauna, the arrival of European settlers was the decisive factor in the decline of many of the species native to the continent. When the Europeans came they

found the dingo, a wild placental dog, but that animal was almost certainly introduced by aboriginal man. The new settlers brought domestic dogs, cats, and pigs with them; rats and mice escaped from ships. Sheep and cattle came; European red foxes and, later, rabbits scourged the countryside. Domestic animals became feral and further destroyed the natural balance. The rifle and shotgun became major factors. The fur trade was established and land was plowed. In short, with the coming of the white man—the spoiler—the Australia of the marsupial ceased to be. The continent became a zoological no-man's-land, suspended on the brink of disaster.

No less than thirty-seven Australian mammals seem to be in trouble today. Some of these priceless creations may already have

been hopelessly decimated. Others are certainly too far gone. Some few may yet be saved.

Nowhere else on earth are there marsupial animals like those in Australia: those marsupials that exist elsewhere (in South, Central, and North America) are considerably less significant to the faunal picture of their respective native regions. The situation in Australia and the small land areas near it is very bad indeed. At least eleven species of Australian marsupials have become extinct since Europeans arrived, ten of them since 1901!

One of the most interesting cases in the sad story of Australia is the Tasmanian pouched wolf or tiger, also called thylacine. *Thylacinus cynocephalus* is the largest and most formidable living marsupial carnivore, assuming that it is still living. Some writers refer to it as the most perfectly adapted carnivorous marsupial.

During the Pleistocene epoch, the thylacine was common, it is believed, over much of Australia. For uncertain reasons the animal disappeared from this range. It is often suggested that the dingo, a far more adaptable, far smarter animal in direct competition with the thylacine, was largely responsible for its demise on the mainland.

All the thylacines left in the world today, if there are any, live within or near an area of 300,000 acres east of Macquarie Harbor in the western part of the island state of Tasmania. In a rugged land, this area is even more rugged by comparison.

No one knows how many of these strange creatures are alive. There may be only a dozen or fewer, or the thylacine may be already extinct. In 1930 one was shot. In 1961, one was seen. Those are the last two substantiated reports. Some tracks have been noted, and some casts made as well, but just the two specimens verified.

As early as 1863 the extinction of the thylacine in Tasmania was predicted. Until very recently it was considered vermin there, and from 1888 until 1909 there was a government bounty of one pound for each adult and ten shilling for each immature specimen caught or killed. It is reported that between 1888 and 1914, 2,268 of them were taken. There was a rapid decline in numbers after 1910, and there may have been an outbreak of a disease capable of decimating the population in that year. The decline since then, has been steady.

The thylacine is very doglike and is a perfect example of parallel development. It has doglike dentition set in a doglike skull; it stands like a dog and has the habits of a nocturnal canine hunter. The sixteen to eighteen chocolate-colored stripes that mark its lower back led early settlers to refer to it as the "zebra opossum" or "zebra wolf." The animals hunted alone or in pairs. They attacked wallabies, rats, birds, smaller marsupials, and possibly lizards. Unfortunately, they also began raiding stock, and sheep and poultry farmers suffered.

The Tasmanian Wolf or Thylacine

Very little is known of the breeding habits of these predators, but it has been reported that three or four young are carried for about three months in the pouch, where there are two pairs of nipples. There are no thylacines in zoos today and no records of any having been bred in captivity. Many years ago, a few of the larger and more impressive big-city collections had thylacines, but today even good photographs of living specimens are rare!

How much sheep farmers actually suffered from the depredations of the thylacine will never be known. Farmers tend to exaggerate their predator problems, but where domestic sheep are raised the wildlife balance has been so altered that domestic animals often fall prey to predators. However innocent or guilty the thylacine may have been, thousands were destroyed by guns, traps, and poison in retribution. Although this was no doubt a major factor in their demise, it was not the only one. The imported placental animals, witty by comparison, pressed hard as well. With so much wildlife destroyed that hunting became increasingly more difficult, with attacks on livestock bringing ever harsher vengeance, the thylacine was doomed.

Those 300,000 acres in rugged western Tasmania should be maintained as a preserve where a lonely pair or two of these ancient creatures may yet mate and produce an occasional litter. Perhaps, if there are any left (it has been several years since a verified sighting, and that was the first in thirty-one years), a small population, inbred though it would be, might be re-established.

The Guadalupe Fur Seal

AMONG THE Pinnipedia, the world's seals, sea lions, and walruses, there are a number of fur seals of the genus *Arctocephalus*. The South African, New Zealand, Australian, Kerguelen, and South American fur seals are all found south of the equator. One species alone ranges today into the northern hemisphere, the Guadalupe fur seal, *Arctocephalus philippii townsendi*. A close relative, *Arctocephalus philippii philippii*, from the Juan Fernández and Más Afuera Islands off the coast of Chile, is apparently extinct.

The Guadalupe fur seal is a solid-looking animal, although it is not big, as seals go; the male can weigh as much as 300 pounds and be six feet in length. The color over all is blackish gray, and the snout is adorned with rusty brown splotches on the sides and quite distinctly yellow whiskers. They are slow breeders, the females delivering one pup every other June.

The Guadalupe Fur Seal

At least four or five times during its bizarre history in the last century and a half, the Guadalupe fur seal has been thought to be extinct as well. In fact, it is making a slow comeback from the verge of annihilation. As recently as 1948 the species was listed as probably extinct. Then, in 1949 and again in 1951, a lone bull was seen in the company of some sea lions on San Nicolas Island, and in 1954 the momentous news was broadcast that fourteen animals had been found in a cave on Guadalupe Island. There may be as many as five hundred in the world, although that figure seems a little high.

The seals were formerly found as far north as the Farallon Islands off San Francisco and from there south to Santa Barbara, San Nicolas, Santa Cruz, Santa Rosa, San Miguel, Ventura, Guadalupe, and San Benito Islands. Today, only the seventeen-square-mile, sun-baked, rocky Guadalupe Island off Baja California has any population at all. They share the island with a Mexican weather station.

Author Peter Matthiessen tells a bizarre tale that seems characteristic of the animal's recent career. In 1928 a fisherman by the name of William Clover sold a pair of bulls to the San Diego Zoo. Becoming enraged over a payment dispute, he vowed to destroy whatever was left of the world's population and managed to kill sixty specimens before perishing himself in a saloon in Panama, where he had gone to sell the hides of his victims.

The Guadalupe fur seal was subject to the same dreadful carnage that has pursued fur seals for centuries all over the world. Particularly during the nineteenth century, they were slaughtered for their hides and for oil. In 1806, 8,338 skins were taken on San Benito Island. In 1810, eight men killed 33,740 animals on the Farallon Islands. They came back in 1811 and took 21,153; in 1812 they took 18,509. In a three-year period these eight men killed 73,402 fur seals. Little wonder the species had all but vanished from the Farallons by 1826.

In the south, the slaughter was even more appalling. In a seven-year period, 3,000,000 Juan Fernández fur seals were killed on Más Afuera Island alone. At one point no less than 1,797 hunters from fourteen different ships were on the island. The subspecies there, as we have noted, is apparently extinct. By the end of the nineteenth

century the fur seal industry from San Francisco southward no longer existed.

The slaughter of the fur seal off California and Baja California was not solely the work of Americans. The British were there; and the Russians had a station in the Farallons from 1812 to 1840, taking Aleut slaves with them from their great settlement on Kodiak Island to do the slaughtering for them. They retreated toward the north only after it had become painfully apparent that the game was up: the fur seal population had collapsed under the onslaught.

There is no data to indicate that the Guadalupe fur seal ever bred in captivity, and there are no specimens in zoos today. Whatever is to be done to preserve the species will have to be done in the wild, by the Mexican government. There is nominal protection for them on Guadalupe Island, but it should be made far more stringent.

The rocks on Guadalupe Island have been worn smooth by millions of hauling-ups by fur seals. Amid the rock jumble along the shores that rise starkly from the Pacific Ocean, the slaughter sheds can still be found, grim reminders that commercial destruction of animals will continue wherever the law will allow or whenever the law can be avoided. Great and valuable animals from the sea have long attracted man. Whales, sea otters, seals, sea lions, and walruses have all been hunted assiduously. Man has profited from all of these, wiping out many without regard for the future or for simple humanity. There are reports that today baby fur seals in the Pribilof Islands are skinned alive to avoid marring the skin with a death blow. Can this be true in the last half of the twentieth century?

It will probably be a long time before simple humanity will be cause enough for man to abandon a fashionable or profitable industry. But the reduction of marine mammals is fast progressing to a point where it is no longer profitable to continue the hunt. Perhaps simple economics will save the remaining species. Still, the record is a bad one and not one we should be allowed to forget. Surely, the Guadalupe fur seal can stand as a symbol for the rest. He has survived not through the mercy or even the common sense of man but through the tenacity of life and the skill of our mother the sea in keeping secrets.

The Blue Whale

THERE is no mystery attached to the tragic decline of *Sibbaldus musculus*, the blue whale, the largest animal the world has ever known. Without regard for the simplest rules of economy or common sense, much less humanity, men have hunted this animal to the very brink of extinction, and this after more than ample warning. Unlike so many endangered species, the whale lives in an environment that man cannot yet alter. The animals themselves, though, are vulnerable.

The earliest written records of whaling activities date back to A.D. 1250, but long before that men had learned how to slay the smaller whales and had discovered what treasure lay in the whale's blubber and good red meat. No one can say for certain who was the first to hunt whales, but for many centuries it was strictly a coastal industry. Eventually, men learned to handle large ships on heavy seas and whaling grew into a major industry, with whole cities built on the profits.

The serious decline of whale stocks began in the 1860's with the invention of the harpoon gun and steamship. Factory ships, speedy catchers, radio, sonar, radar, helicopters, and a number of other modern devices have been added since, and whaling is not only a fine art today but one self-doomed to prompt destruction.

Modern whaling is limited almost exclusively to the Antarctic. There are small coastal whaling activities spotted around the globe, but the great seas bordering the six-million-square-mile Antarctic continent are where the bulk of the industry now concentrates its efforts. Truly modern operations began there in earnest in 1904, with the establishment of the first station on South Georgia Island.

Some idea of the growth of the industry after the establishment of the modern shore stations on those remote subantarctic islands can be gained from a few statistics. The figures show the blue whale kills for the years indicated:

Year	Location	Blue Whales Killed
1909–1910	South Georgia	26
1911–1912	South Shetlands	892
1925–1926	South Shetlands	2,157
1926–1927	South Georgia	3,670

The world-wide kill of blue whales shows how this upsurge in whaling activity has affected the world's population of the animal:

Year	Blue Whales Killed
1929–1930	19,080
1955–1956	1,987
1962–1963	208
1963–1964	112

The 112 kills made in the 1963–1964 whaling season resulted from sixteen Antarctic whaling expeditions: seven from Japan, four from Russia, four from Norway, and one from the Netherlands. The drastic drop can be attributed in part to regulations set down by the International Whaling Commission. But more important, the blue whale, as a species, is on its way out. The blue whale (also known as sulphur-bottom, Sibbald's rorqual, and great northern rorqual) will probably be the first species of whale made extinct by man. Other species have been greatly reduced in number by the slaughter, but none, as far as is known, has been pushed to total extinction.

The International Whaling Commission meets annually to set standard kill limits for the following year. This standard is stated in "blue whale units." A unit is equivalent to one blue whale or two fin whales or two and a half humpback whales or six sei whales. Each week the catch is radioed into the Bureau of International Whaling Statistics at Sandefjord, Norway. As the season progresses

the weekly reports become daily. When the total number of units allowed for the season is reached, the season is closed. In the 1963–1964 season we discussed earlier, a total of 8,429 blue whale units were taken, of which only a hundred and twelve were actually blue whales.

The blue whale, the most valuable animal on earth, has been steadily declining not only in numbers but in over-all economic significance. In the 1931–1932 whaling season, 82.1 per cent of the catch was blue whales. Blue whales now account for less than 5 per cent of the catch, again in part due to whaling restrictions. The figures have been so convincing that since 1953 special restrictions have been put on blues, allowing their hunting only toward the end of the season in the Antarctic. Since 1960 they have been afforded virtually total protection in the North Atlantic, where they are excessively rare.

The Blue Whale

The blue whale is an amazing creature. It can be well over a hundred feet long (although the average is less) and can weigh up to 160 tons or more. A newborn calf is twenty-three to twenty-five feet long and can weigh more than an adult elephant.

While most of the remaining blue whales live in the southern hemisphere, the species can properly be said to summer near the edge of the Arctic and Antarctic ice packs. In winter they head for subtropical waters to bear their young. They generally avoid the real tropics. They usually travel alone or in pairs, seldom in large pods like some other species.

Blue whales are not fast breeders. There is usually a two-year interval between pregnancies, with gestation running about eleven months. Single births are usual, twins apparently rare. The calf will nurse a full seven months and is said to require at least a ton of milk per day. According to available knowledge, females are able to breed in their fifth summer. The life span is probably close to fifty years.

The swimming pattern of the blue whale is quite regular and facilitates their slaughter. The whale takes a deep dive of ten to twenty minutes' duration, then surfaces before taking a number of shallow dives lasting twelve to fifteen seconds each. Cruising speed is ten to twelve knots, although fifteen can be attained if needed. It is quite easy for the modern whaling fleet to take advantage of this rhythm and be waiting for the unsuspecting animal to surface. Helicopters circle overhead and radio information to the catchers, while the invisible fingers of sonar probe into the gloom and bounce back with vital secrets to the ships at the surface. Even if aware of its enemies, the blue whale is doomed. Swim as it will, it will soon be exhausted and make ever shallower dives. Finally, it lingers at the surface one moment too long and the explosive harpoon hurtles through the air to crash into flesh and end the great, wild life.

Where does the blue whale population stand today? In 1930 there were between thirty and forty thousand still swimming in the world's seas. By 1953 the estimates were down to nine to fifteen thousand. By 1962 some estimates were below a thousand, and below seven hundred by 1963. These are only educated guesses. The sea can still keep secrets, even thousands of them!

There are, of course, more stories than one to tell when we deal with as complex an international enterprise as whaling. Here, at least, men were not slaughtering animals for the joy of it. Whaling was very big business and very hard work. It was also terribly important to a protein-starved world. Whales can properly be thought of as a harvest, a natural and legitimate economic resource. The whaling ship, as such, cannot be condemned unless the slaughterhouse and butcher shop be damned as well. The literally hundreds of products from the hundreds and thousands of tons available from a good whale season were in the past vital to human welfare and progress.

It is over now for the hunters of the blue whale; the great reduction in numbers in the last thirty years has made these great creatures the scarcest of the large whales. When hunting the blue whale is no longer possible, the other great species will each in turn be reduced to the point where it makes no sense to hunt them. A whaling fleet from Norway, Japan, or Russia cannot afford to travel all the way to the Antarctic to catch possibly a few whales.

Since man has failed so far to exterminate a known species of whale, perhaps the blue whale will survive. When it is no longer economically feasible to join the chase, perhaps the killer ships and factory ships will retire and the few whales left will start back up the painful trail to recovery. Or perhaps the few remaining whales will be so scattered that they will fail to breed. No one knows.

Even when the intentions of whaling men have been good, the sea offers special problems in conservation. Mistakes are easy to make. In the nine years from 1949 to 1957, 31,305 blue whales were taken world-wide. Of these 1,195 were undersized and illegal and 92 were lactating females. Those 92 females probably meant 184 blue whale deaths! In the 1931–1932 season, only 8.1 per cent of the blue whales taken were sexually immature. By 1955–1956, 39.8 per cent of the blue whales taken were too young to have bred. These "infraction" statistics would be tolerable in a stable population. But the blue whale is on the very brink of disaster. To destroy a single female and leave her calf to die of starvation is a tragedy.

There are enigmas when we examine the whaling picture. Children starving for protein cannot be ignored, but neither can the simple fact that these children will soon be denied whale meat as well. Man has been extremely foolish in his attitudes and actions. Individual whalers have ignored the rules. Meetings of the Commission have degenerated into political displays, endless debates, and open denial of the very principles and purposes behind them. Greed, avarice, utter stupidity—these have been the weapons with which man has set the fate of the world's mightiest creature. The harpoon gun and the flensing blade have been secondary.

Soon they may be gone, these incredible animals whose world is so foreign to our own. The paintings of them, the legends, the unsatisfactory photographs will all still be here, but not the animals themselves.

The Tuatara

THE NAMES Stephens, Stephenson, Cavalli, Little Barrier, Great Barrier, Mercury, Mayor, and Motiti mean a great deal to the herpetologist and conservationist. They are eight of the approximately twenty rocky islets that cluster near the shores of New Zealand's two main islands and the home of one of the most interesting animals still alive on this planet.

Long before the remarkable spread of the dinosaurs, back in the Triassic and Jurassic periods, at the very beginning of the great age of reptiles, there lived and flourished an order of reptiles known as the Rhynchocephalia, the beak-heads. They appeared in South Africa, in southern South America, and across Eurasia. They were of moderate variety in shape, and one species at least grew to be six feet long.

Then the reign of the dinosaur began. As the dinosaurs grew in size and variety, the beak-heads began to vanish; species after species disappeared from area after area. The great dinosaurs thundered across the land, and the beak-heads seemed to shrink before them. In due time, reckoned in scores of millions of years, the dinosaurs also vanished, relinquishing the rule of the primeval world to the warm-blooded mammals. However, after the last dinosaur gasped away its life in some long-vanished quagmire, a beak-head

species lived on, as it does today, on those twenty or so little islets off North and South Islands, New Zealand. They are indeed living fossils; they were here before the Rocky Mountains and, by millions of years, before the genes leading to man could be formed in a living creature.

The tuatara, *Sphenodon punctatus*, the last of this ancient order of beak-heads, is not a beautiful creature. Up to thirty inches long (but only rarely), brownish in color with a yellow spot on each

scale, it looks like a stout lizard and lives on insects and possibly sea bird eggs.

The tuatara is a slow breeder. As many as fifteen eggs are deposited in a shallow nest and covered by the female in a final parental gesture. The nest is then abandoned. Fifteen months later the eggs hatch. Growth is painfully slow, and two decades may pass before sexual maturity is reached.

There is no doubt that the tuatara once ranged over the two main New Zealand islands. There has been no verified record of any mainland population in historical times, however, and it does not seem that man or his feral animals played the major part in the creature's decline. It is likely that a long-range weather change was involved, with a resultant alteration in the relationship with local plant and animal life.

There are probably well over ten thousand specimens left on the islands today, perhaps even fifteen thousand, so the mainland population must have once been immense.

The New Zealand government is very proud of its tuataras, and positive measures have been taken that may well serve as an example for the rest of the world. Not only is it against the law to capture or kill one of these reptiles; a special permit is required for a scientist even so much as to set foot on one of their islets to look at them. To pick one up is to break the law. Nor are these regulations only theoretical, as are many others elsewhere; they are rigidly enforced by the sensible New Zealanders.

Some specimens have done well in captivity, in one instance living for half a century. In 1963 the world-wide captive population was eight specimens in five zoos. In 1965, there were six in five zoos. Since New Zealand is so strict about its charges, few will reach zoos in the years ahead. Speculating in tuataras is not a safe commercial venture.

Is there any danger? There is. It would take a careless human race little time to destroy ten to fifteen thousand little lizardlike animals, which serve no economic role. "Why allow twenty pleasant islets to remain the sole property of a bunch of scaly reptiles? We are so overcrowded, why not populate those fine, sunny offshore pieces of land?" people may one day ask. Stranger things have happened to animals far kinder to the eye than the tuatara. Then, of course, there are such modern necessities as naval gunnery practice, missile bases, lighthouses, weather stations, fisheries, and canneries.

As long as man is man, the tuatara will bear watching. No animal is more vulnerable, and few more ancient. The one category requires our pity, the other our respect. Perhaps, in this case at least, we can appreciate both.

The Galápagos Tortoise

AT ONE TIME great tortoises of many species ranged across Europe and North America in uncounted numbers. They were the direct descendants of animals that had arisen before the dawn of the great age of reptiles. Slowly, over the millennia, the range of the world's giant tortoises shrank until, by the dawn of historic times, only the desolate Galápagos Islands astride the equator five hundred miles off the coast of Ecuador in the Pacific Ocean, and the Seychelles, Aldabra, and Mascarene island groups in the Indian Ocean had any specimens. The rest of the world had only fossil records.

These isolated colonies of ancient animals could almost certainly have continued to thrive, were it not for man's interference. The populations were huge. On Rodriguez Island alone, in the Indian

Ocean, thirty thousand tortoises were killed in the one year 1759–1760. Predictably, there were none left on the island a hundred years later. It is estimated that more than one hundred thousand specimens were removed from the Galápagos Islands by American sailors between 1832 and 1862.

The Galápagos Islands were discovered in 1535 by the Spanish explorer Fray Tomás de Berlanga. Early visitors found the giant members of the family Testudinidae so plentiful that they eventually named the island group after them, *galápago* being the old Spanish name for "tortoise." When the islands were first visited by Charles Darwin three hundred years later, he marveled at the great creatures and found them still quite plentiful.

But where hundreds of thousands of these giants once roamed in stolid peace, few or none remain today. In the Galápagos group, Chatham, Hood, Charles, Barrington, and Jervis Islands have been stripped; the subspecies once found on these islands are extinct. On Indefatigable or Santa Cruz Island, between one and two thousand at the very most may survive. There are some on Albemarle Island, but they are seriously threatened and may not survive. Narborough may harbor a small population in the interior, but the area has seen recent volcanic activity and the subspecies once reported from there may be gone.

The decline of these giants can be attributed to two causes: the giant tortoise, despite its size, is defenseless against imported predators and competitors, and it makes excellent eating.

It is difficult at first to accept that an animal with a shell more than a yard across, more than eight feet in circumference and weighing more than five hundred pounds, can be victimized by a rat, dog, cat, pig, goat, or cow, but such is certainly demonstrably the case. The Galápagos Islands did not have a mammalian population before man imported one. Rats escaped from his ships, dogs and cats ran wild when abandoned, and whaling ships left cows, goats, and pigs to establish feral herds that could be called upon by passing vessels. The pigs and rats attacked the eggs; dogs, cats, and rats attacked hatchlings, and cows and goats joined the others in destroying fodder and water supplies. The ancient tortoises were not equipped by their millions of years of isolation for such fast-moving company. They could only decline in direct proportion to the competition.

The second prong of man's attack was much more direct. In the days of sailing ships, the lack of fresh food was a pressing problem. A certain amount of livestock was carried to be slaughtered on long crossings, but the supply could not be large because of the fodder required to sustain it. The giant tortoise supplied the perfect solution. If a tortoise's shell is not damaged, and if the temperature is satisfactory, it can live a year without food or water, so at least the old reports state time and again. During the seventeenth and eighteenth centuries, ships would put into the Galápagos before attempting a Pacific Ocean crossing or before heading south around Cape Horn. They would fill their holds with giant tortoises—fourteen, fifteen, or more tons at a time—and sail off with a living larder requiring absolutely no care. The animals were slaughtered as needed, the meat they provided reportedly better than either chicken or pork. Early settlers on the islands frequently lived for months at a time on these giants, leaving their shells empty and bleaching by the thousands.

Nor, unhappily, is it all over yet. Ecuador has passed laws protecting the unique fauna of her island possessions but has done far too little to uphold her own regulations. Young tortoises are still carried off regularly for sale to tourists ignorant of the harm caused by the trade they are supporting. Ecuadorians still slaughter the tortoises for their meat and oil; in a one-week period in 1960, ten fresh carcasses were found within a small area where the creatures were already approaching extinction.

The practice of using the tortoise as a source for oil grew up in the nineteenth century when American whalers would stop on the way home and collect a few hundred tortoises. Each adult, we are told by the numerous records, would yield about three gallons of clear oil when rendered. Wandering freely among the tortoises as they grazed on their scrub and cactus, killing the animals at will and with ease, must have appealed to sailors weary after long months at sea and dangerous encounters with infuriated giants of another sort. The carnage was incredible, and subspecies were wiped out on island after island.

The Galápagos Islands, because of their isolation and peculiar volcanic character, developed over the eons into one of the most perfect evolutionary laboratories on earth. The iguanas, the fourteen species of Darwin finches, the flightless cormorant, and the tortoises all demonstrate in textbook fashion the processes described by Darwin after he visited there in the nineteenth century.

Today, unless Ecuador tightens her controls and unless conservation efforts of massive proportions are launched immediately, the islands will lose their incredible fauna. Areas should be isolated where predators can be removed or destroyed. Subspecies should be transported to competition-free areas where, hopefully, some can survive. It will probably not be possible to hold some of the sub-

species distinct because remaining populations are so extremely small that they may need to interbreed in order to survive at all. Efforts to save the giant tortoise must, however, remain speculative until further studies are financed and completed. The Charles Darwin Foundation, established in 1959, is dedicated to this cause.

The giant tortoises do surprisingly well in captivity. In 1964, there were approximately 192 specimens of the Aldabra tortoise, *Testudo gigantea*, in sixty-six zoos. Four of this number were hatched in captivity. In the same year, there were 185 of the various Galápagos tortoises in seventy-one zoos. The breakdown, according to the *International Zoo Yearbook*, was:

Subspecies	Number of Specimens	Number of Zoos
Galápagos	88	29
Testudo elephantopus elephantopus	(21 hatched in captivity)	
South Albemarle		
Testudo elephantopus vincina	26	7
Chatham Island		
Testudo elephantopus chathamensis	3	3
Abingdon saddleback		
Testudo elephantopus abingdoni	2	2
Duncan saddleback		
Testudo elephantopus ephippium	5	3
Hood Island		
Testudo elephantopus hoodensis	2	1 (San Diego)
Porter's black		
Testudo elephantopus nigrita	18	8
Testudo elephantopus incerta	1	1 (Frankfurt)
Beck's saddleback		
Testudo elephantopus becki	1	1 (Bronx)
Unidentified subspecies	39	16

Prior to 1961 there were just eight recorded hatchings in captivity. In that year, twelve eggs were laid in the San Diego Zoo, and after 174 days four of them hatched.

This list of captive specimens demonstrates that it is not only possible to maintain these animals in zoological collections but to do so in some cases while maintaining the integrity of subspecies. This will enable specialists to study the processes of evolution as pictured in these living textbooks long after the islands from which they came have been swept clean of any life worth studying. It may be that, in the final analysis, the zoos of the world are the only places where they can survive. A great deal of study is called for. Here, once again, time is running out.

The Komodo Dragon

Since the early 1920's, adventure-story writers have had a grand time with the great lizard known popularly as the Komodo dragon. The name was apparently too good to resist. The Komodo dragon, the largest species in the suborder Sauria, is the world's largest living lizard. It can grow to ten feet in length, although this great size is found only in males and that not very often today. All fanciful tales to the contrary, maximum weight probably never greatly exceeded three hundred pounds.

The Komodo dragon is impressive in size and aggressive in disposition. Despite this, it is readily identified by a number of physical characteristics as a member of the family Varanidae and so is nothing more than a large monitor lizard. There are twenty-three species of monitors in the world today, ranging from the eight-inch western-Australian species *Varanus brevicauda* to this monster from Indonesia, *Varanus komodoensis*.

Monitor lizards were once found around the world but are now strictly old world in distribution. They are quite dragonlike in appearance, having a long head and neck, a heavy, rather short body, a thick, long, and powerful-looking tail, strong legs equipped with sharp claws on each toe, and a very long, snakelike, forked tongue. Popular fiction writers have added the fire breath and an occasional hint of man eating.

The dull brown or black Komodo dragon may have come to Indonesia from Australia, descended as it appears to be from a form now extinct on that subcontinent. Since all the monitors are power-ful swimmers and since the Torres Current is conveniently eastward in direction, an island-hopping migration is not altogether to be dis-counted. But however the dragon came to its present home, and however long ago, that home is very limited in size now. At one time *Varanus komodoensis* was found on Komodo Island, Rintja Island, and a limited part of Flores. These are in the formerly Dutch Sunda Islands. They may have once been found as well on Poeloe Padar Island, but this has not been substantiated. Today, only Komodo and Rintja Islands have any dragons left. There are perhaps three hundred in all, and most of these are on Komodo Island.

Komodo dragons prefer the open, rather bare hills to be found on parts of these tropical islands. They will go into light forest land but are most content in areas of alang alang grass and in very light brush. Like all other monitors they are scavengers, seeking endlessly for carrion. They are large enough to hunt for themselves, though, and will not hesitate to do so. They will take what they can get, depending on their size; the largest specimens will take young deer and wild pigs. Interestingly enough, they have no natural enemies, which probably explains why they survived into modern times in their remote island homes instead of becoming extinct like their cousins, the other giant monitors, in other parts of the world.

Since they are not preyed upon, even by man, they will maintain themselves as long as their habitat and the natural prey populations are not cut back or seriously disturbed.

Unfortunately, other hunters move through the grass, brush, and forest lands of twelve-by-twenty-mile Komodo Island. Natives from nearby Timor, starved for protein as are nearly all the people of Indonesia, come to the home of the dragon and seek its prey. Pigs and deer carried off and thus denied to the dragon spell its doom, for it is too big as an adult to survive on the birds' eggs and beetles that sustain it when it is young. Unless a nature preserve is fast established that will protect the prey of the Komodo dragon as well as the dragon itself, it will become an extinct species much sooner, perhaps, than many of us would care to believe. The Dutch, wise in the ways of the world, passed the first laws protecting the Komodo dragon in 1926. They did not see then that the pigs and deer of the lizards' island home were what needed watching.

In 1964, there were sixteen Komodo dragons in zoos around the world, plus an unspecified number in the Jogjakarta Zoo on Java Island. There is a report of a breeding in an Indonesian zoo during World War II, but no information is available. If the Komodo dragon is to survive, it will not be in zoos. It must be left in the wild state, where people care enough to make simple provisions for the largest lizard left on our planet.

The problem of the Komodo dragon raises a large issue, one we really must face in many parts of the world. Are the natives of Timor to be denied access to desperately needed meat to save the lives of three hundred lizards that have no economic significance? Are three hundred lizards worth the life of one human child? Superficially, the question seems to be, which comes first, people or lizards? But if the Timor people are permitted free range on Komodo Island, they will soon wipe out the entire pig and deer population. Komodo Island is not a reliably permanent larder. The Komodo dragons will vanish, and the people will move on to new areas, equally hopeless for sustaining anachronistic hunting and fishing cultures in our age. The world is no longer suited for hunting and fishing peoples to

carry on their ancient economics. They live a pitiful existence for their efforts, far below the standards of the rest of the world.

Despite romantic notions to the contrary, in many areas the survival of wildlife will be possible only by the elevation of the living standards of the indigenous peoples. In this context, wildlife conservation is seen as a part of a much larger picture. Man and wildlife will move forward together or, in many areas at least, not at all. We—those of us who are smug enough to believe ourselves to be on a higher plane of social development—come from long lines of despoilers. We had better pass our hard-earned lessons on to the innocents of the world before they finish what our forbears started, the ultimate destruction of the wildlife of the world.

The Eskimo Curlew

THE FAMILY Scolopacidae of the order Charadriiformes organizes, into one logical group, eighty-two delightful wading birds of predominantly northern distribution. The subfamily Tringinae contains the tattlers, curlews, godwits, and willets. Three other subfamilies contain the snipes, woodcocks, sandpipers, turnstones, surfbirds, plovers, stilts, lapwings, and oyster catchers, among others. It is a handsome, busy, and everlastingly interesting group of feathered creatures that add life and excitement wherever they appear.

The Eskimo curlew (*Numenius borealis*), the smallest of the American curlews, seldom exceeded thirteen or fourteen inches in length. Despite its small size it engaged in an annual migration of heroic proportions. It bred on the open tundra well beyond the tree

line in the northern Mackenzie District of Canada. It is possible that some bred farther west, perhaps as far as Alaska, although that information has not been generally accepted by ornithologists. Specimens were seen in Alaska during the last century but no nesting sites were identified.

In late summer, the great migration began. While a small number headed south over the Great Plains, most set a course east across North America to Labrador. From Labrador and Newfoundland they headed south, touching the American coastline only at Long Island, New York, where they were known as "futes." On their departure from New York they headed once again over vast stretches of open water, occasionally being seen at Bermuda and in the West Indies. Still pressing southward they crossed the coastline of South America, ending their monumental flight on the campos of Argentina.

When severe storms coincided with these southbound journeys, many were undoubtedly lost at sea. Five times stragglers were found in Scotland and Ireland; each occasion coincided with a severe storm or hurricane. In the south, stragglers were seen as far to the east as the Falkland Islands and as far to the west as Peru and Chile.

After the winter months, the great flights of curlews again headed north but over a different route. They left Argentina in late February and early March, reaching Texas and Louisiana by mid-March. From there across the lower Mississippi they flew, north over Missouri and Kansas, Nebraska, Minnesota, and the Dakotas. Flying in a loose wedge, flocks ranged in number from three thousand to some so large the count could not even be guessed.

Wheeling beautifully, opening and closing formation in great swirling gyrations, their fluttering whistle heard far below, these gregarious and trusting birds were well known wherever their route took them over inhabited land. They would come to earth in great flocks for the night before again heading off on their flight.

In the middle of the last century these flights still contained vast numbers of birds. Up through the center of America they went, by the tens of thousands. By 1890, they were scarce. By the early 1900's they were a thing of the past. What happened?

The Eskimo Curlew

There is a slight possibility that some unknown factor was involved in the tragic decline of this handsome species. There could have been a disease at the nesting grounds; there could have been an extremely unfortunate juxtaposition of circumstances such as a series of summer Arctic storms while the newly hatched birds were still unable to fly. Such unknown factors have often been suggested; but, as far as can be discerned from available evidence and well-recorded facts, the Eskimo curlew was simply slaughtered until there were no more left to kill.

In the middle of the United States, the Eskimo curlew was known as the prairie pigeon or the doughbird. It was, unfortunately, delicious eating; and the slaughter for market was appalling, more than any species could long endure. In American history, and perhaps in all the heartless story of man against nature, the bloody history of the Eskimo curlew is second only to the story of the passenger pigeon. Masses of gunners would assemble along the flyway and blast upward into the flocks for hours. A dozen or more birds could be had for a single shot shell if the gunner waited until the birds were in the right position overhead. They were carried off to market by the wagon load to be sold for a few pennies apiece. Thousands were left to rot where they fell. Thousands more, it is reported, were fed to pigs.

This mass overshooting probably explains the decline of both the passenger pigeon and the Eskimo curlew. These are just two more cases where man saw natural resources in apparently limitless quantity and felt that his demands could never outstrip the supply. It has happened with timber, on almost every continent, with water on most continents, and with wildlife nearly everywhere on earth man has ever trod.

In a way, the first part of the story is understandable. In those days, literacy was not universal, and communications were extremely primitive: the governor of a state did not fly over troubled areas in a helicopter and return to address his constituents on television. Tens of thousands of people, particularly in rural areas, never read a newspaper. The farmer in Nebraska who shot two hundred curlews before breakfast did not know where they came from and did not know where they were going. He neither knew nor cared how many there were in the world. He only knew that they came each year and blackened the sky overhead. His shot shells, if not home made, were very inexpensive, and both his family and his hogs needed food. He could, as well, earn a few very easy dollars by selling some barrels of curlews in the town market.

What cannot be understood is why such men continued the slaughter when it became obvious even to the least informed that the birds were fewer each year. Why did these men continue to shoot when the birds were overhead in flocks of a few dozen and not thousands? What happened to the farmer's natural sense of economy?

The position of the Eskimo curlew is not clear today. There were sightings and even some specimens shot (!) in the early and mid-1930's. Almost every year since then, scattered reports have claimed that a few curlews have survived, but most of the sightings have been discounted. Two were reported heading north near Galveston, Texas, in 1945. One was reported in 1959, one in both 1960 and 1961, and two in 1962 from the same area. There have been more recent reports, but most conservationists just shake their heads or shrug. They simply don't know.

There are no known breeding grounds. It has been decades since a nest was last seen. The Eskimo curlew, although smaller, resembled the Hudsonian curlew. Without the two birds to compare, even a practiced eye could mistake the two, even though there are distinctively different color markings on *borealis'* wings. No one has had much practice at watching Eskimo curlews for a long, long time!

The species is probably not yet extinct. Perhaps they do breed in extremely small numbers in a hidden, perhaps even unmapped spot along the Arctic coastline. Perhaps these few migrate by routes unknown to us. Fortunately, habitat destruction did not play a part in the decline, so the physical conditions necessary for survival still exist. The sea otter lived through apparent extinction, as did the Guadalupe fur seal. If the survival of the species can be demonstrated, it will be a red-letter day for conservationists, for perhaps with the total protection it now enjoys the species can rebuild itself.

The Everglade Kite

NATURAL overspecialization may account for the long list of animals great and small that vanished long before man arrived on earth or during the long periods when he was too few in number and too limited in skills to do any real damage. Even without the destructive hand of man, history has seen an endless coming and going.

Whether or not these are mistakes on the part of nature is actually something of a philosophical question. It could be argued that this is the way things are supposed to be; some species, perhaps even all species, are temporary and must eventually give way to inevitable successors. Perhaps there are no ultimate evolutionary goals. At any rate, when nature does allow a species to become overspecialized, that animal is condemned to eventual extinction, for overspecialization presupposes that surroundings will remain constant. Since there are no real constants in environment except perhaps for parts of the ocean and the atmosphere, the results of being unable to adapt are death not only for individuals but for species, entire genera, families, and even orders. This is what probably happened to the dinosaurs and the hundreds of species—mammals, birds, and reptiles included—that followed.

There is an excellent case in point in our own time. The noisy, even raucous Everglade kite or snail hawk, *Rostrhamus sociabilis*, is overspecialized to the point of being doomed, at least in the United States. This member of the family Accipitridae, subfamily Milvinae, was probably never found north of Tallahassee Bay, Florida. From there it ranged southward through Mexico, Central America, Cuba, and deep into South America. Throughout this vast area the bird could eat only one food, the snail *Pomacea*. Its narrow, sickle-shaped bill was adapted to this one diet item, and its habits, too, were built around the search for this one life-giving substance.

The Everglade kite was once found throughout southern Florida's endless acres of fresh-water marshes, where *Pomacea* abounded. Then, starting around 1895, man drained the marshes for agriculture, for animal husbandry and, finally, for the vast multimillion dollar recreation industry. As the marshes dried up and became loudly touted vacation paradises, never-ending citrus groves, and cattle ranches, the *Pomacea* became fewer in number, and so did the kites. They could eat nothing else. Eventually, the snails concentrated in the drainage ditches that helped prevent the marshes from reclaiming their own, where a parasite that infects these snails, the lung fluke, increased in incidence. The parasite was passed along to the kites that now were forced to feed along these ditches, and the kites died in turn. The same thing may be happening in Cuba.

There is no longer any question of the Everglade kite surviving in the United States. They will not. Today, it is America's rarest bird, with probably fewer than a dozen alive. They will survive in Mexico, possibly in Cuba, and certainly in Central and South America for a while longer. For years and even perhaps centuries yet, this kite will gather in colonies of from twenty to a hundred and hunt *Pomacea* at dusk and at dawn. In mercifully obscure Central and South American marshes the nests will still be built, and the two to four white eggs marked profusely in several shades of brown will continue to hatch. But some day the sound of the bulldozer will be heard and another habitat will fall. Man's population is blossoming, and vast tracts of submerged land cannot be tolerated forever. Such land areas are needed and will be claimed.

Hope lies in the belief that awakening mankind will set aside virgin samples of each kind of habitat left on each continent of sufficient size to allow the rare and the tormented to live on as examples of the past. This kind of preservation is the Everglade kite's only chance for survival, for otherwise all of its habitat will one day vanish and time and the lung fluke will have their way.

Man has helped the kite toward extinction in other ways, too. Egg collectors have ruined nests that couldn't be spared, and the kite's resemblance to the marsh hawk has brought undeserved fire-power into play. More than one duck hunter has eased his boredom by cracking an Everglade kite out of the sky.

Certainly, man has caused the downfall of this rare and interesting animal. Is cause the same as blame, however? Should man not have drained the Florida marshes to put the otherwise economically valueless land to use? Man, too, as a species must survive, and if he can make a fertile and productive land of a vast marsh, he must. He should also, though, leave something as it was. Perhaps he can learn in time to do it in Central and South America.

This gives rise to problems that are international in aspect. Man did not practice sane conservation in Florida despite the affluence of twentieth-century America. Can it be expected of him locally in poverty-ridden areas farther south? I do not think so, not realistically. International bodies with international sources of revenue must step in, not to criticize but to legally acquire land that can be set aside, with the guidance of experts from all over the world, for the perpetuation of habitats and species. Each nation, surely, must be ultimately responsible for its own natural housekeeping, but we

cannot wait for universal maturity and affluence. Surely it will come, but it will come far too late for dozens and perhaps hundreds of species. Until this great day arrives, preservation must be the work of such scientific bodies without artificial boundaries as the World Wildlife Fund. The United States cannot in any kind of sense or conscience turn to Venezuela or Brazil and say, "You save the kite—you pay for the swamps." Colombia cannot say to Mexico, "You save Baird's tapir, we need the virgin climax forest." India cannot turn to Kenya and say, "You save the lion." These problems are international and, within the context of each nation's laws, each nation's needs, guidance and money must be available. Without this universal flow of the necessary ingredients of conservation, very little is going to happen in comparison with the staggering needs of wildlife at this very moment.

The Monkey-Eating Eagle

THE WORLD has 289 species of hawklike birds and 133 species of owls. Taken together these magnificent birds are popularly known as raptors, the birds of prey, and they belong to two orders: Strigiformes, the owls, and Falconiformes, the eagles, hawks, kites, falcons, buzzards, condors, and vultures. One of the great families of the Falconiformes is Accipitridae with its subfamily Buteoninae, containing the eagles, including the crested, the harpy, the golden, the imperial, the martial, and the bald; the sea hawks; some of the buzzards; the hawk eagles; and many of the most dramatic hawks.

Pithecophaga is a genus of this subfamily with but one species, *P. jefferyi*, the awe-inspiring monkey-eating eagle of the eastern Philippines. This great thirty-six-inch bird is listed by the IUCN as rare and is today found only on the island of Mindanao. While some reports suggest that there are one hundred wild specimens left, in fact there may be fewer than fifty.

One of the largest predatory birds left in the world, the monkey-eating eagle is admittedly of somewhat frightening aspects. White, cinnamon, and dark brown with a few black markings, this bird has a great crest of feathers around its head that looks rather like a fright wig. Its eyes are intense and staring and, as it flies overhead (it does less soaring and more flapping than many other eagles), it emits a strange wailing cry that inspires neither love nor poetry.

As its name suggests, this great hunter eats monkeys, which it snatches from the high trees along the mountain slopes that it favors, and hornbills, and it readily invades native villages to take small animals. It need hardly be stressed that it is not beloved by the native population. This offers particular problems in its preservation.

Its horrific name and its almost as horrific appearance make this bird a favorite zoo exhibit. In fact it is generally suggested that the excessive trapping of zoo specimens is a major factor in its recent decline in the wild. There are seventeen known specimens in twelve zoos at the present time, and all of these were taken from the dwindling wild stock. There are no recent records of captives breeding.

The monkey-eating eagle does not reproduce rapidly even in its natural environment, and although two eggs are generally laid, rarely is more than one young seen at a nesting site. It is possible that the weaker of the two young produced is used to feed the stronger. The nests are almost always found in giant kapok trees in the least accessible rain forest and mountain areas.

The education of native peoples is essential if this great bird is to survive many more years, but education is not easy. A great bird with a powerful beak and talons that appears out of the sky like an evil spirit does not inspire sympathy. When it steals dogs or livestock, it becomes an enemy. The sight of it snatching a monkey off a branch to kill and devour by tearing apart does not add to its popularity.

The raptors have been etching their designs against the clouds since the Cenozoic era, for some thirty-six million years, and have a very real place in the economy of nature: they are, as are all predators, cullers of surplus and removers of inferior specimens.

The monkey-eating eagle is not the only bird of prey to lack the love and sympathy of local populations. Around the world the raptors are persecuted and hunted by every possible means. The great golden eagle is in dire straits and in North America is hunted from airplanes by sheep farmers. The bald eagle may become extinct unless drastic measures are taken and elsewhere in the world, on every continent, species after species is being pushed to a point where survival is highly questionable. It is going to take understanding and a far more mature appreciation of nature than is now generally found if these predators and their four-footed mammalian counterparts (not to mention the reptilian forms) are to survive. Is a thirty-six-million-year-old life form to be ended now by our prejudice?

The habits of these animals, specifically of these birds we call raptors, are not particularly attractive. They are killers—often enough, killers of animals we either need for our own uses or prefer over the birds themselves. On the other hand, they are also killers of uncounted millions of rodents each year. Nature, we see, is quite capable of arriving at a balance, and in areas where she is allowed to do this without interference of man, she and her progeny do well.

The raptors are a valuable form of animal life, not only to the scientist, who has more than a passing interest in such successful life forms, but to the farmer, rancher, and city dweller, who otherwise might be overrun by rodents or would pay ever-increasing food costs because of farm losses to skyrocketing rodent populations.

Admittedly, the monkey-eating eagle probably plays no significant role in the economy of the Mindanao natives, nor is it likely to do so for any such population in the foreseeable future. It is, in fact, in the rather unfortunate position of being something of a relic, only a case in point for raptors in general. It would be a great pity, though, for this fascinating creature to pass into oblivion.

The Whooping Crane

A GREAT DEAL of interest in the plight of wildlife has sprung up in the United States and Canada in recent years. In no small part this concern is a direct outgrowth of public sympathy for the magnificent, stately whooping crane, *Grus americana*.

In ancient times, this great crane wintered from Florida to California. Before the middle of the nineteenth century they were still found on the wing from the Arctic Circle to central Mexico and from Utah to South Carolina. These five-foot-tall birds, with their great seven-foot wingspread, were probably never very numerous. In historical times the population may never have risen above fifteen hundred, according to some educated estimates. On many counts this aggressive species is painfully vulnerable, and they have not done well in the face of marching civilization. The advance of agri-

155

cultural demands and the draining of wetlands and coastal marshes have been exceedingly harmful. But man and his guns have been the whooping crane's greatest enemy.

Whooping cranes are slow, heavy flyers and cannot be considered good wing shooting by any real sportsman. Yet they have been shot very nearly out of existence; they are so large and so handsome overhead that men with shotguns have found it impossible to resist taking a passing shot. The tallest, most stately bird in the United States and Canada is almost certainly doomed to extinction as a result of this destruction.

Conservationists have been following the fortunes of the whooping crane carefully for a number of years. In a very real way, this great white bird with his red face and black-tipped wings has become the symbol of conservation in the United States. The count of wild birds in some sample years has been:

Year	Number of Birds
1938–1939	18
1941–1942	15
1949–1950	34
1952–1953	21
1956–1957	28
1958–1959	33
1959–1960	36
1960–1961	38
1964–1965	42

There are, as well, at the time of this writing, seven specimens in two zoos, bringing the 1965 total up to approximately forty-nine living specimens. This is not a very promising set of statistics.

In 1937, when concern for the species began to mount, the 47,000-acre Aransas National Wildlife Refuge was established on the southeast coast of Texas, seventy-five miles north of Corpus Christi. Arriving in October, all of the world's known whooping cranes winter at Aransas until mid-April, when they begin their two-thousand-mile northward migration. At Aransas they are both studied and guarded. An oil company agreed to restrict its drilling operations in the area, and the Air Force agreed to cancel bombing practice on nearby Matagorda Island in deference to the concern of conservationists.

The migration which begins in mid-April in southern Texas carries the birds in pairs or small bands across Texas, Oklahoma, Kansas, Nebraska, South and North Dakota, Montana, Saskatchewan, Alberta, and to the southern shores of Great Slave Lake in Canada's beautiful Wood Buffalo National Park situated in the Mackenzie district of the Northwest Territories.

In 1945 the Cooperative Whooping Crane Project was set up by the U. S. Fish and Wildlife Service and the National Audubon Society. Refusing to subscribe to the theory popular among some groups that the bird was senile and doomed no matter what was done, the project directors set up a program of study and public education. It is this program that has awakened millions of Americans and Canadians to what is happening to their wildlife. It also established the whooping crane as the best-known endangered species on the North American continent.

It is a bit of blind good luck that the remaining flock breeds in a Canadian national park. No doubt other flocks bred both east and west of the park; had the Aransas flock been wiped out by a hurricane, as happened to the Louisiana flock, and had another flock been the only surviving one, the species might be extinct today.

What has been causing grave concern among conservationists is not the crane's security at either end of the migration route but what happens to it during its monumental four-thousand-mile round trip between these two points. There is, on an average, a 30 per cent loss during migration, half of this from shooting. No fewer than twenty-four specimens were shot during migration between 1950 and 1953. A refuge is urgently needed along a fifty-mile stretch of the Platte River in Nebraska where the migrating birds concentrate. If the trumpetlike call of this species that can send shivers down men's spines is to be heard a few years from now, educational activities started in 1945 must be intensified to the point where every man, woman, and child likely to lift a gun along the flyway will

know the bird on sight and understand how tenuous its hold on life is. There is now a great deal of public sympathy, to be sure, but not enough.

The breeding potential of the whooping crane in captivity is apparently good. A captive breeding program such as the one that restored the Hawaiian goose and Przewalski's wild horse as viable species must be instituted. Only about four young a year are produced by the wild flock, and that is not enough! The species is doomed unless this natural propagation is augmented by a comprehensive captive program. One hurricane on the southeast coast of Texas before April or after early October could spell doom for the species in minutes, for this tall bird could not avoid the storm by flying away or by crawling into some natural shelter.. An outbreak of disease or any other seriously disruptive influence in the area of Great Slave Lake could similarly spell immediate disaster. The flock is far too small and far too restricted in the two ranges at either end of its migratory route. It will not survive unaided. Sooner or later, something is bound to happen to make either its summer or winter range unsuitable, even if only for a short time. There is, too, the danger of a violent storm along the migration route. Spring

into early summer, late summer into early fall, the birds are on the wing across the Great Plains. A tornado could bring extinction if gunners do not.

Some people have pointed out, and not without logic, that a disproportionate amount of publicity has been given to the whooping crane. Although it is one of the rarest birds in the world, its plight is no more worthy of public attention and concern than that of the California condor, the Javan rhinoceros, or the orangutan. Still, symbols are necessary to attract attention to a portion of the problem that the public can focus on. The whooping crane, the great educator, has provided the necessary focal point. From it people are learning just how perilous the entire wildlife situation is, and from this starting point, views may broaden to encompass all the rest.

There have been some who have felt that too much time, attention, and money were being spent on a doomed species. These are not just pessimists but very active, often malicious people. One group of farmers in Saskatchewan, for example, vowed to kill every whooping crane they saw and put a quick end to the species and to the expensive attempt to rebuild it. It is men such as these who have caused the disastrous destruction of natural life around the world. Perhaps education will eliminate their kind before they bring an end to our natural world.

The California Condor

Six raptors, the birds of prey, belong in the order Falconiformes, family Cathartidae; these are the six species of new world vultures, each of which has its own genus. There is the great Andean condor (*Vultur gryphus*), the king vulture (*Sarcoramphus papa*), the black vulture (*Coragyps atratus*), the turkey vulture (*Cathartes aura*), the yellow-headed vulture (*Cathartes burrovianus*), and one of the largest flying birds that has ever lived, the giant California condor (*Gymnogyps californianus*).

The giant condor of California's coastal ranges and interior valleys comes to us carrying the secrets of the Pleistocene epoch in its avian brain and blood. It has been described as "living ecology," a living link to the world of the saber-toothed tiger, the mammoth, the mastodon, and the short-faced bear.

The California Condor

A long time ago, probably back in Pleistocene days, the California condor, or a close relative, ranged eastward across the United States to Florida, where its bones have been uncovered. In recent times it has been seen alive as far to the north as the Columbia River in Oregon. It vanished from Oregon no earlier than 1860. Even as recently as a hundred years ago the great bird, with its nine-and-a-half-foot wingspread, probably bred in nearly all of California's many mountain ranges. Then something happened.

Today there are probably not fifty California condors left in the world. All that survive center on two protected areas in two California counties. The Sisquoc Condor Sanctuary, near Sisquoc Falls in Santa Barbara County, is the area where most survive today. It covers some twelve hundred acres and surrounds one of the last-known nesting areas. It has been protected since 1937. The other sanctuary is in Ventura County.

Both directly and inadvertently, man is responsible for the decline of the California condor. While great flights of these enormous birds never darkened the sky as did those of the passenger pigeon, there formerly were many, many more than there are today.

Although huge in size and equipped with a powerful ripping beak, the condor does not hunt; it is a scavenger. It must look for dead animals and feed on their carcasses. A basic cause of decline has been the destruction of native wildlife. Great herds of elk (wapiti), deer, pronghorns, and other large game animals once roamed the areas over which these twenty-pound birds soared majestically. Then man came, not only with guns but with cattle. Fewer cattle were to be found dead than the predator kills and other remains of wild animals, but still the condor got by in somewhat reduced numbers. Then fruit farms replaced ranches. The result was disaster for the big birds. Food was short, probably always short, and the condor numbers diminished, increasingly aided by the ubiquitous rifle and shotgun. There is, however, no evidence that a food shortage has affected the condor population in recent decades. Although the effect of reduced wild game on the condor population in the past is imperfectly understood, starvation is not recognized as a cause of contemporary condor mortality.

Even with no enemies but man, the condor could not flourish with the ever-increasing pressure of habitat destruction, egg destruction, and hunting; the ancient bird began to fail. At one time the powerful fliers went to the coast and fed on the food treasures thrown up by the sea. In fact, the first written record we have of the species, in 1602, was made aboard ship by a Carmelite friar, Father Ascension; he reported a mass of them feeding on the carcass of a beached whale. Skeletons of the birds have been found far inland with marine shellfish remains included as apparent foodstuff. But the California condor does not go to the sea anymore.

In 1880 a law was passed in California protecting these birds. It was all but totally ignored. In 1963, the California Fish and Game Code, Section 3511, was made to read:

> Fully protected birds are: California condors *(Gymnogyps californianus)*; bald eagles *(Haliaetus leucocephalus)*; white-tailed kites *(Elanus leucurus)*; trumpeter swans *(Cygnus cygnus buccinator)*. Fully protected birds may not be taken at any time and no provision of this code or any other law shall be construed to authorize the issuance of permits or licenses to take any fully protected bird and no such permit or license heretofore issued shall have any force or effect for such purpose.

That, at least, would seem to be clear enough. No one may shoot a condor in California without facing a $500 fine or six months in prison, or both. Yet, in 1963, the year when this law was passed, two condors are known to have been shot. In 1964, one is known to have been shot. Despite sanctuaries and the laws that govern and protect them, despite legal protection of the birds that goes back twenty years into the last century, only one man has been punished for killing one of these rare creatures: in 1908 some poor soul was fined $50 for killing a California condor. That is concrete; the rest has been conversation and some very good intentions. The state government has taken a good many encouraging steps in the right direction, but a substantial part of the public has been unwilling to follow suit.

The California Condor

There are probably no more than eight nestings a year now among the remaining condors. Each female lays one egg, four and one half inches long and two and one half inches in diameter, on the bare floor of some high mountain cave or in the open among a pile of boulders. Rarely a second egg may be laid particularly if the first is lost. Incubation takes forty-two days, and the young are wholly dependent upon both parents for a full seven months and partially dependent for another seven. This is a dangerous state of affairs. If anything should happen to one parent, there is the danger that the other will not be able to feed itself and the chick with the reduced food resources throughout the area. The birds breed every other year and must be five or six years old before they breed at all. This, too, is a dangerously low reproduction potential.

With a population of under fifty to start, with only eight possible breedings a year, with some attrition from natural causes, with men still shooting at them, and with traps set for other animals occasionally catching one, the California condor has little chance of seeing the dawn of the twenty-first century.

Fortunately, it is doubtful that poison baits set for ground squirrels, coyotes, and other pests are responsible for as many condor deaths as was once thought. They have strong constitutions, for although they seem to prefer fresh meat they can eat very rancid flesh with no ill effects.

The sanctuaries that exist are under constant pressure from various groups, as might be expected. California condors are so near destruction, many argue, that it is silly to ask man to sacrifice his interests to preserve them. The birds should be written off, conservationists are advised, and only incidentally the land allotted to them should be given over to stockmen or oil and mineral interests. Even mass recreational planners, people who should be sympathetic to the problems of conservation, are drumming their fists on the gates.

The powerful California condor has only one superior. He will give way at feeding to a golden eagle. Otherwise, he is king of the skies in those few areas where he still exists. Perhaps that is why men want to shoot him down.

There have been excuses given for killing the condor, of course. Any number of stockmen, even today, believe that the condor kills livestock, particularly newborn lambs, calves, and foals. They are a little stuck when asked to name a date and a place or to lead you to the scene of such an atrocity, but still they believe it. Tell them, show them even, that the condor has the foot of a turkey, not an eagle, that it has nails and not talons, and still they won't believe that these birds are scavengers only.

"If condors aren't killers, they are at least carriers of many dread diseases!" You will hear that often enough, until you ask for evidence. Then, of course, you get a shrug. It is a totally invalid claim, without scientific foundation.

There were other, more honest, reasons in the old days that helped destroy these great birds. Their giant quills, used by miners as tubes for carrying gold dust, were a standard container, holding ten cubic centimeters when fitted with a wooden stopper. Many condors, perhaps many hundreds, were killed for their quills. We are told, too, that many were captured by early settlers and used in a form of cockfighting, often pitted against golden eagles.

Men have killed California condors in pits over screamed wagers; they have killed them for their quills, and because of ignorance of their habits, and certainly idiotic men and boys have taken and smashed their rare eggs. But most of all, men have shot them because they are big and wonderful and alive. An adult overhead with the great white flashes beneath his wings is a wondrous sight, a thing that fills the sky. What power some men feel when they can snuff out such a life! How simple to fold the wings of an animal whose race is almost incomprehensibly ancient and which is not very much smaller than the greatest bird that ever flew. How wonderful is the power of man, and how lucky it is that nature gave us intelligence with which to guide our actions and a heart with which to judge them.

Steller's Albatross

EARLY in the last century more than a million magnificent white albatrosses winged their endless way from Kamchatka to the southern coast of China, from Alaska to California. The great Steller's albatross, *Diomedea albatrus*, with its seven-foot wingspread was a welcome sight to any sailor at sea. Travelers on the Pacific Ocean could depend on seeing some every day between July and October, no matter how far from land they were.

Several evils, both natural and unnatural, have befallen this species, until today it is one of the rarest birds in the world. In 1957–1958 there were thirty-five known specimens; sixty-five in 1961–1962; in 1962, they were badly hit by a typhoon, and their present plight is uncertain.

The unnatural evil was the feather trade. That murderous enemy of all bird life accounted for almost endless slaughter. It is reported that over a half million of these handsome birds were clubbed to death on their nests between 1887 and 1903 to satisfy the incredible vanity of the human race. Unable to grow feathers of their own, humans slaughtered endlessly to acquire the unnatural decoration. Whatever one wants to think about the wearing of furs, at least they keep people warm. But feathers! If it were not so tragic, it would be funny.

The Steller's albatross has bred in historical times on many small islands along the Asiatic coast, but the largest and most important colony has apparently always been on Torishima, in the Seven Islands of Izu, the Bonin group, Japan. Today, the only known breeding colony, a pitifully small one, is to be found on Torishima. The birds spend a very long time at their breeding colony, from September until July, so they are most vulnerable there. They lay only one egg per year per pair, and a third of the chicks are killed by eagles and crows each season. Reproduction at best has its difficulties.

The range of the albatross today, since it is an oceanic species, can only be guessed. One may have been seen off California in 1946. One may have been seen in the southwest Pacific, somewhere between New Guinea and the Caroline Islands in 1951. A few may breed on some small islands off Formosa. Very few acceptable reports of sightings have come in in the past few decades. The species appears to be doomed.

The more natural evils that befell this bird during its terrible decline are the result of the volcanic nature of Torishima. In 1933 and again in 1941, eruptions very nearly wiped the species out completely; most of the adults were killed and no eggs or chicks survived. Still, the damage done by feather hunters by wiping out other smaller colonies was even more destructive.

Before 1900 there were fewer than fifty human beings living on Torishima. That was enough, though. They attacked the birds on their nests with fierce determination and regularity. Each man could kill one hundred to two hundred birds a day without really exerting himself. All the humans on Torishima were killed in a volcanic eruption in 1903, but more came.

By 1929, there were only two thousand specimens left in the once-vast colony. In 1932, cattle were introduced onto the breeding range, and in December of that year the inhabitants of the island launched a massive assault for the feather trade. In that one month they killed three thousand birds, the species having recovered slightly in the preceding three years. With men clubbing the adults to death and with cows blundering onto eggs and chicks alike in search of fodder, the bird all but gave up. In 1933, fewer than one hundred appeared on the island, and the decline has been steady ever since.

Hunting has been forbidden on Torishima since 1906, but this has meant absolutely nothing until quite recently. A special decree by the Japanese government in 1957 made Torishima a special

reserve, reaffirming the older no-hunting admonition. Still, it is the end of the feather trade and not the laws of Japan that will offer Steller's albatross this respite. It is unlikely that the species will survive either way. It has been pushed too far.

It is impossible to think of Steller's albatross and then, quite naturally, of the egret in Florida without feeling regret at being part of the same animal species that engaged in the feather trade. By the millions, magnificent feathered creatures were slaughtered so that women could parade in mock splendor. Unfeeling men waxed fat on this traffic in death and misery. Part of that feather trade has been legislated out of existence. (Some wardens and conservationists were actually murdered by feather hunters in Florida!) Other parts of the business are inactive simply because the mode is not with us at the moment. But if some designer brings out his next spring collection bedecked with plumes, every conservationist in the world must rally to protect the world's bird life. Stores offering styles that involve feathers other than ostrich plumes (these farm-raised birds may suffer slight indignities but are not killed for the plucking) must be told in no uncertain terms that they are on a blacklist that will materially affect their sales for as long as they continue to encourage such insupportable barbarism.

The killing of birds for their feathers is not in any way parallel with the killing of livestock for food. There is not a shred of necessity in the feather business; it is one of the greatest evils man has perpetrated against our natural world.

The Hawaiian Goose

THE STORY of the Hawaiian goose or néné (nay-nay) is one to cheer any conservationist or nature lover. What began as a tragedy ended as a signal triumph of sense and reason.

We can conjecture that about a half million years ago some geese migrating southward stopped on one or more of the Hawaiian Islands. The biggest island, Hawaii, was already more than a half million years old at that point, and Maui even older. Whether due to injuries, storms, or forces and factors we cannot guess, part of the flock remained behind and, in isolation, developed into a distinct species. Their relationship to the Canadian goose (*Branta canadensis*) is not difficult to establish, but *Branta sandvicensis* is clearly a goose apart.

The Hawaiian Goose

We do not know what islands of the Hawaiian chain they inhabited and we do not know what their maximum numbers were, but by 1780 reduction at the hands of man had begun. The néné makes delicious eating, and whaling ships began stopping by to load up with barrels of salted goose carcasses. The birds are not shy by nature and were extremely easy to hunt.

Hunting is not the only weapon in man's arsenal for species destruction. Capturing live birds and taking eggs were just as effective. Explorers and exploiters flushed the birds from their ground nests, and sandalwood gatherers continued the work. Beach resort development and ranching began to limit the birds' habitat. Military roads cut into the interior, bringing more men and havoc.

Two special factors played hand in hand in the near destruction of this species. The néné does not migrate and probably has never left the Hawaiian Islands since its emergence into a distinct species. Also, and perhaps more importantly, it has moved inland away from the coast. It lives and breeds on open lava floes where some of the twenty-nine known plants in its diet grow. It is therefore particularly vulnerable to predators. It has a slight vertical migration, up in the spring, down in the autumn.

When man began settling these lovely islands, he brought with him many foreign life forms that helped destroy the once great flocks of these large and handsome birds. Mongooses, rats, dogs, cats, goats, sheep, cattle, horses, pigs, asses, at least six different game birds, and many foreign plants were introduced. All of these conspired to destroy nests and young birds, as well as adults, competed for habitat, and destroyed or competed for food. The isolated néné was not equipped to survive. As a matter of record, all the bird life of Hawaii suffered terribly. Sixty per cent of the Hawaiian bird forms, including at least twelve distinct species, have been exterminated.

By the early 1800's there were still 25,000 néné left, and few people gave the plight of the species much thought. The first specimens reached Europe in 1823 and were successfully bred in captivity. The last descendants of these birds died in France in 1940.

The Hawaiian Goose

In 1911, a rancher, Herbert C. Shipman, deeply concerned for the fate of the species, began raising the birds in captivity at his home at Keaau on Hawaii. The Hawaiian Board of Agriculture and Forestry began raising them in 1927. In 1935 they set forty-two specimens loose, but all but one of the descendants of these birds had died by 1949.

In 1951 two females and one male (two of the birds from rancher Shipman's stock) were sent to the Wildfowl Trust at Slimbridge, England. By 1958 this flock of three had increased to seventy-three, testifying to the skill and dedication of Peter Scott and others involved in this marvelous venture. As protection against the accidental loss of the flock through disease or other misadventure, breeding pairs were sent to wildfowl centers in Holland, France, Switzerland, other locations in England, and to the care of Dr. S. Dillon Ripley in Connecticut.

The World Wildlife Fund in the United States then financed the transfer of thirty specimens from Slimbridge to Maui Island, where none of the species had survived, if indeed any had ever lived there. Haleakala crater had been declared a national park by the United States government, and the area was considered a safe place to start the birds back on the road to recovery in their natural surroundings. A small wild stock had survived on Hawaii itself and may have numbered thirty-five birds. In 1955, a wild flock of twenty-two geese was sighted. It was the first time in nearly two decades that more than eight were ever seen at one time. By 1962, the néné world population had increased from the fifty that were alive near the turn of the century to over four hundred. By 1965 the number had passed five hundred, and, with constant vigilance, the species will survive.

Although hunting of the néné was forbidden as far back as 1911, it is clear that the species could not have survived without this concerted effort on the part of individuals like Shipman and organizations like the Wildfowl Trust and the World Wildlife Fund. To save the world's wildlife, more is needed than asking hunters to put up their guns.

The Hawaiian Goose

It seems certain now that the thin *uck-uck* call of the flying néné will continue to be heard in the Hawaiian Islands generations hence. They will nest in the grasslands and open forests, in open country up to 7,500 feet, and in woodlands to the edge of the rain forests. Although we do not know what other islands they reached in the past, new colonies will be established along the chain to ensure the species' chances. There are nearly 150 of these somewhat quarrelsome geese in nearly twenty zoos and collections, and from this stock new blood can be added to those already back in the wild.

Survival of the néné has taught us what can be done when man brings his sciences to play on constructive projects instead of destructive ones. For wildlife can be a focal point for stimulating and wholesome interest and recreation. We should teach our children to hunt with cameras, not with guns, and teach them that the natural world is their heritage and responsibility.

The Indian Pink-Headed Duck

No ONE can say for certain why the strange and not very graceful Indian pink-headed duck *(Rhodonessa caryophyllacea)* has vanished, but such is apparently the case. Somewhere, along the banks of a hidden pond deep in an area of high grass and dense bushes, somewhere in Oudh, Nepal, Manipur, or Assam or somewhere in between, a pair may yet live on and possibly even nest, but for all intents the species is gone from this planet.

This rather odd-looking duck was related to the pochards, but ornithologists realized this only recently. The pochards are of worldwide distribution and number fifteen species, including the canvasbacks, the scaups, and the white-eyes. Off to the side of the family tree was the pink-headed duck, although he did not dive as the true pochards do. He was not a percher either and was seldom seen in association with other species. Small groups of six or eight of these birds were seen on rare occasions in the first decades of this century, when they were still hunted in Bengal. Occasionally a bag of six or more in a day were taken, and they were seen in the marketplace from time to time. About a hundred years ago they were quite common, particularly in the duars of eastern Bengal. They were often seen during tiger hunts, when the elephants carrying the hunters drove through deep grass in pursuit of the great striped cats. They

were shy, secretive, and little known. Seldom were they seen except on these chance encounters.

The pink-headed duck apparently was really quite rare by the end of the 1920's. They had once ranged north to the Punjab and south along the coast as far as Madras. The center of their distribution was north of the Ganges and west of the Brahmaputra River, including the areas of Purnea, Malda, Purnlia, Bhagalpur, and Tirhut. They must have been reasonably common at one time for they had many names: they were *saknals* in Bengali, *dumrar* in Nepalese, *lal-seera* or *golablal-seer* in Hindustani, and *umar* in Tirhut. They had been known to science since 1790.

The areas from which the pink-headed duck came are remote, and often underdeveloped. No one will say when the last low, wheezy call of the male was heard, or the last time the distinctive bright-pink head was seen bobbing up and down in the grass near a remote pond whose waters the duck had to share with crocodile and tiger. If anyone knows, they have not heard that the information is very much desired by conservationists. The last authentic record of a wild bird came from the Darbhanga district, Bihar, in 1935. The last captive bird in Europe died sometime between 1940 and 1944.

From time to time there was apparent confusion on the part of some observers between the pink-headed duck and the red-crested pochard *(Netta rufina)*, which is also found in India. There should have been no problem in identifying the pink-head, though, for he was quite awkwardly distinct. He had a narrow bill, a long and extremely thin neck, quite long legs, a thick body, and a short, unimpressive tail. The male was adorned with a bright rose-pink bill, head, and neck while his body was basically a brownish black. The female's pink parts were less impressive, with a dull whitish overcast. They reportedly nested from April on and the egg was quite uniquely almost spherical in shape, white or pale yellow in color.

During the years when they could still be found in the wild, the Indian pink-headed duck was also found in captivity. The Calcutta Zoo generally had a few pairs, and specimens were shipped to faraway zoos as well. Shipments reached London in 1874 and again in 1897. Darien, Connecticut, had at least one in 1912, and Surrey, England, secured three pairs in 1925. The birds got along well in captivity, were hardy, lived a decade or more, and did not fight among themselves or with other species, but they did not breed. There is not a single recorded case of a nesting in the confines of a zoological collection, and no specimens exist in captivity today.

In years past, surely, thousands and perhaps millions of people have looked casually at a pink-headed duck or two as they passed the waterfowl enclosures of this zoo or that. In a marketplace somewhere in the middle of Bengal, perhaps a wife and mother reached up and pressed her thumb hard into the blackish breast feathers of a strange-looking duck hanging by its feet. Perhaps she took it home, plucked it, and cooked it for her family. No one seemed very concerned. With or without a pink head, a duck is a duck unless someone stops to look, to think, and to ask questions.

Now, almost certainly, the Indian pink-headed duck is gone, the victim of man's indifference. Perhaps he was an antique species, or one in an evolutionary cul-de-sac. There have been many of these. However, by whatever means and from whatever causes, this is yet another species quietly gone away forever and one less chance for man to preserve the world around him on anything even remotely resembling the world that once was. A lost species is indeed a lost chance.

Attwater's Prairie Chicken

AMONG the brilliantly feathered panorama that is the world of bird life is an order known as Galliformes. Its members are variously referred to as fowl, game birds, or gallinaceous birds. It is a group both useful and ornamental, embracing as it does all of the world's grouse, pheasants, guineafowl, turkeys, brush turkeys, domestic fowl, curassows, junglefowl, ptarmigans, that prime European game bird, the capercaillie, and a strange link to ancient times in South America, the hoatzin.

One of the great families of Galliformes is the grouse family, Tetraonidae. Within this family there is a genus of particular interest in North America, *Tympanuchus*.

The heath hen, *Tympanuchus cupido cupido*, was once found from Maine to Virginia, as far as we can tell. During the early colonial days it provided reliable dinner fare for settlers along the eastern seaboard. It was hunted with ease, and little thought was given to its preservation. A few regulating laws were passed, but they were ignored. Then, quite suddenly, there were none to hunt.

In 1890, a search revealed that there were somewhere between 120 and 200 heath hens living on Martha's Vineyard, an island off the Massachusetts coast. The hue and cry went up, and the birds were declared inviolate. However, poachers still arrived in their punts and whaleboats, feral house cats and dogs still carved away at the small population of ground-nesting and therefore vulnerable birds, and by 1906 there were just 77 specimens left.

By 1908, frantic conservationists coming out from Boston could count only 60 specimens, but the bird then began a comeback. Responding to more stringently applied rules governing their safety or perhaps just answering an ancient population cycle, the population rose to 300 in 1910, to 1,000 in 1914, and to almost 2,000 in 1916. In that year a devastating fire roared through the scrubby undergrowth of the Atlantic island, aided by offshore winds. In 1918 there were 150, and in 1920, 600. The population was too restricted, though, and never really recovered. The area was too small; there was excessive inbreeding and disease, and by 1925, 24 birds remained alive.

From December, 1928, onward, saddened scientists and nature lovers went again and again to the island but could find only one male bird. In April, 1931, on April Fool's Day, this lonely specimen was carefully captured and banded. It was then seven years old and in apparent good health. Naturalists still hoped that a mate survived somewhere out in the scrub brush that would join with this male to keep the species going. Their hopes were unfounded and it died, the last example of a once great and populous form of bird life, on March 11, 1932—or at least that was the last time it was seen alive. The species had been protected by law since 1824. It had been to no avail.

There are other examples of the family Tetraonidae in North America today. There is the sage grouse or sage hen *(Centrocer-*

cus), the sharp-tailed grouse of the genus *Pedioecetes*, and three more members of the genus that once contained the now-lamented heath hen.

The greater prairie chicken, *Tympanuchus cupido americanus*, is found on the northern prairies of Alberta, Manitoba, Wisconsin, Missouri, Nebraska, and the lower peninsula of Michigan. It is the most common and best known of the prairie chickens. The lesser prairie chicken, *Tympanuchus cupido pallidicinctus*, has not done as well and could be in for trouble in the years ahead; it is found only in western Oklahoma, southwestern Kansas, the Texas panhandle, and in adjacent New Mexico. The limits of the former ranges for these two subspecies cannot be defined with absolute certainty, but it is known that they were spread much farther than they are now and in much denser populations. The greater prairie chicken did, we know, extend southward to Texas and eastward to Pennsylvania.

The real cause for concern rests at the moment with Attwater's

prairie chicken, the third living subspecies. *Tympanuchus cupido attwateri* was once densely distributed over large areas in Louisiana and Texas, at least. It may never have spread much farther than that, but there were at least a million specimens in that area according to early reports. In 1937, the count stood at eight thousand. Today there are fewer than fifteen hundred, and it appears as if the bird could easily follow the trail to oblivion laid down by the heath hen.

All living examples of this interesting subspecies can today be found in two extreme southwestern Louisiana parishes, Cameron and Calcasieu, westward into Texas but only as far as the Rio Grande, and thence northward to the vicinity of Austin.

This narrow strip of humid coastal prairie on the Texas-Louisiana state line is the Martha's Vineyard of the Attwater's prairie chicken, and here man will demonstrate whether or not the heath hen has taught him anything.

Two factors played hand in hand to reduce this interesting creature to its present perilous state. Hunting has been a constant pressure and one the bird could not answer with a suitable change in habits. It is nonmigratory and is always found in open grassy areas. It could neither retreat to other ranges nor hide in denser growth and still reproduce itself because of the peculiar nature of its courtship ritual. In former times hunting parties of ten or twenty men would camp for days at a time in the bird's preferred range and hold contests for the largest bag. Without regard for dwindling numbers, these men—out for what they considered a good time at any price—blazed away, often leaving a thousand or more carcasses rotting in the prairie sun when they packed their kits and returned to their livelihoods. The prairie chicken wilted under the barrage. Since the birds spend virtually all of their time on the ground (even in the winter they burrow under the snow at night), they could be easily started with dogs or by men on horseback, and the sport, as it was considered, was the easiest imaginable.

The second great factor in the near destruction of this wonderful subspecies was, predictably, expropriation of habitat. It can inhabit neither true forest nor farmland successfully but must have wild grasslands, undisturbed prairies of tall grasses along the humid coast. It derives most of its food from native plants and only secondarily from agricultural crops. The wild petunia is the most important single item in its diet, followed by stargrass, bedstraw, doveweed, and perennial ragweed. Farm crops of peanuts, hegari, and rice offer some substance but not enough.

Indiscriminate grazing of livestock has reduced the original tall grass areas and allowed the influx of woody vegetation and the unsatisfactory shorter grasses. Agriculture and human industry are further carving away at the former prairie chicken empires. The situation is increasingly alarming.

The courtship of the prairie chicken is too well reported in the nature literature of this continent to warrant retelling here, but the booming, strutting, and gyroscopic aerial displays of the male birds from January to March are a frenzied symphony of sight and sound that is one of the great natural wonders still available for man to watch. For arrogance and fierce masculine pride, few creatures can match the male prairie chicken.

Nesting activity reaches its peak in March. The highly vulnerable nest is a shallow depression in the prairie lined with plant materials and feathers from the adults. Twelve eggs are laid and incubation lasts for about twenty-four days. Egg fertility is very high, more than 95 per cent. If the first nesting is successful, there are no others for the female until the following year. Some researchers suggest that there may be a second if the first fails.

Nesting mortality is high, as it is with all ground-nesting birds. As many as 70 per cent will fall to feral cats and dogs, coyotes, skunks, weasels, ravens, owls, eagles, and hawks. Flooding during heavy rains can be another hazard. A female that has five young by her side come autumn has had a highly successful nesting year.

Ideal population intensity in good range is sixty-five birds per square mile. With this in mind, and using the results of intensive studies that have been made of food and cover requirements, it is possible to save Attwater's prairie chicken from following the heath hen into oblivion and reducing living members of the genus to two. If we fail here, he will almost certainly fail as well with the greater and lesser prairie chickens when their turn comes.

There should be restocking and rigid protection, the development of suitable cover, and the replanting of food crops. We must be ready to provide winter feeding should it become necessary.

The World Wildlife Fund had advocated the purchase of an ideal habitat in Colorado County, Texas. The prairie chicken is using 2,980 acres of original coastal prairie and 440 acres cultivated for rice. This land should be bought, patrolled to keep predators down to a minimum (at least until the birds have rebuilt their populations), and held for all time in sacred trust as a stronghold for a magnificent bird that will otherwise surely vanish in just a few years. As we have seen again and again in the last century, many animals cannot adapt. Man can, however, so the responsibility for these weaker creatures rests with him.

The Notornis

BEFORE the coming of man, first the ancient and obscure moa hunters, later the Polynesian maoris, and finally the white Europeans, New Zealand was the home of some of the most unusual birds that have ever lived on this planet.

The two main islands and the myriad smaller islands and islets had no mammalian fauna to speak of; birds inhabited the ecological niches that were the provinces of furred animals in other parts of the world. Without four-legged predators to concern them, and without snakes to disturb their nests, the birds of New Zealand in an extraordinary number of cases surrendered the power of flight and became swift runners instead of fliers. Some grew to heroic proportions. The twenty-two species of moas ranged from turkey size to the giant *Dinornis maximus*, which stood an estimated thirteen feet tall. The mighty elephant bird weighed close to half a ton and stood nine feet fall. There were five species of the swift-running littl kiwis (there are three species left, all in danger), flightless geese, a wren that almost certainly did not fly, and an eagle that probably could not fly as we define the word.

This wonderland of bird life was absolutely dependent on its isolation. Nothing in its experience enabled it to compete with alien animal forms. Then man arrived with his dogs, cats, rats, goats, pigs, and other domestic stock. Homesick for his hunting ranges, the white settler imported deer, elk, and hoofed animals of many other species from many parts of the world. Without a thought for the magnificent living museum of bird life around him, he brought in the very creatures that could forever destroy it. Devastation was the result.

It is very difficult to trace the record of species destroyed in New Zealand because of the extreme remoteness of its high mountain valleys and relatively sparse population. Birds thought extinct have suddenly reappeared, and birds thought to be in fair condition have turned out to be seriously endangered. We do know that two of the five kiwis are gone, *Cnemiornis*, the flightless goose, and all of the great moas, although there is just the slightest possibility a smaller species of this great group persists somewhere in New Zealand's many secret places; a partridge is gone, three rails, a duck, a flightless wren, a honey eater, and probably the wattled crow as well. At least four species have become extinct in the last century alone, and eight have been found to be in very serious danger.

Every so often in the annals of natural history a really happy event occurs to help offset the tragedy that is all around us. Such was the case with the takahe or notornis.

A form of this flightless turkey-sized bird was known from North Island and another from South Island. In the early years of the nineteenth century, both were thought to be extinct, being known only from remains found in swamps and caves. The form once found on North Island is still believed to be extinct, but the

South Island form, *Porphyrio mantelli* or *Notornis mantelli*, depending on your choice of authority, proved to be one of the great riddles of the natural world.

In 1849, a large, blue-headed, green-backed flightless bird with a bright red bill and shield was killed at Duck Cove on Resolution Island close to the southwest coast of South Island. Incredulous scientists finally identified it as an example of the notornis or takahe. The bird was not extinct!

Two years later, in 1851, another specimen was taken on another island, Secretary Island, not far off the same shore. A search was launched, but no new specimens could be found. Once again a saddened scicentific world declared the species finally done. Then, in 1879, north of the Mararoa River flowing into the western end of Lake Manapouri, just forty-five miles east of Secretary Island, another lone specimen was killed. This treasure finally reached the Dresden Museum, only to disappear during World War II.

The search, launched with renewed fervor, failed to turn up another example of the species, and once again it slipped onto the list of animals made extinct by the settlement of man and his disturbance of natural balances. Then came a miracle: in 1898, a dog killed a fine specimen on the south shore of middle fiord on the western shore of Lake Te Anau. Again an unsuccessful search was launched and again the species was listed as finally, irrevocably extinct. For fifty years, from 1898 until 1948, matters thus stood and then the ultimate miracle occurred: after a half century of oblivion the notornis reappeared, not as a single specimen but as a stable breeding population.

It is a testimony to the wonderful, wild nature of much of New Zealand that Notornis Valley did not even appear on the maps until the rediscovery of the notornis in 1948. Known from maori tradition only as a name, Kahaka-Takahea, "nesting place of the wanderer," this important valley 2,600 feet above sea level had remained in safe and splendid isolation. There, in the Murchison Mountains, five to ten miles west of Lake Te Anau where the 1898 specimen had been killed, the valley and the takahe had remained hidden from man and destruction.

The Notornis

Related to the rails and gallinules, a member of the order Gruiformes, the takahe or notornis although very rare probably has a stable population today. In 1949–1950, twenty breeding pairs were counted, plus approximately fifty nonbreeding individuals. The only immediate threats seemed to come from imported deer, which might destroy eggs in their ground nests as they passed through the area, and from stoats, imported weasels, which in the absence of small mammals to hunt probably press the grounded takahes and their young very hard. If the species is to be saved these stoats are going to have to be removed from the valley, but that is no easy task.

The takahe nests on open ground with a light cover of grass and low brush very close to a lake, marsh, or stream. It runs very well but cannot outrun so determined a pursuer as a stoat. The breeding season apparently runs from October to February, when one to four eggs are laid. Many of the eggs are infertile and may reflect a senility that is dangerous in itself.

There may be a few other small valleys in the Murchison Mountains where the takahe survives, and the ever-alert Wild Life Section of the New Zealand Department of Internal Affairs has established a 400,000-acre sanctuary including the all-important Notornis Valley. The New Zealanders, though few in number, have shown a fierce determination to protect their incredible wildlife treasury.

During a recent visit to New Zealand I stopped one afternoon for tea at a magnificent stone castle that sits atop a hill not far outside of Christchurch. There, in baronic splendor, in what is actually and surprisingly a teahouse known as *The Sign of the Takahe,* I could not help but think back on the story of this strange bird and its incredible game of hide-and-seek with science. It was there, in fact, while reviewing this story, that the idea for this book was born. Here is a rare instance where a remote and little-known bird has shown us what can happen with luck—and with isolation. We cannot offer New Zealand's isolation to many of our endangered species, but perhaps we can learn to be as alert and as intelligent as New Zealand authorities have been.

The Ivory-Billed Woodpecker

IT WILL BE another decade or two before reports of nesting ivory-billed woodpeckers stop coming in from hopeful naturalists and amateur bird watchers, but for all practical purposes, *Campephilus principalis*, the largest North American woodpecker, is no more. It is foolish, of course, to insist that it is all over for a species as elusive as a bird, but it does seem certain that there is nothing left to be done in this case.

Once upon a time, and that not so very long ago, the ivory-bill ranged throughout the river-valley forests of the Atlantic seaboard north to North Carolina, south into Cuba, and westward through the Gulf Coast states to Texas; it extended up the Mississippi Valley to Illinois, Indiana, and Ohio. If any at all survive today they would be found in one of three places: northern Florida, northern Louisiana, or the remotest forests of interior Cuba. It is doubtful that this is the case. A pair was reported from Louisiana in 1946 and another from Florida in 1950. Cuban reports, or at least suggestions, are fairly regular and consistently unreliable. That, in the cold harsh light of our review, is the story of the handsomest and most robust woodpecker of a rich and fertile nation. Time ran out for the species, or there just was no room, or, perhaps, it was a combination of these factors.

There is no doubt that the ivory-billed woodpecker was a senile species. It was successful at a certain way of life—so successful, in fact, that it couldn't adapt itself to any other regimen. When man came along and began reshaping the environment, as he inevitably does, the ivory-bill was doomed. His raucous cry, his beautiful white bill, handsome twenty-inch black and white body, and his bright red topknot were destined for oblivion.

Actually, the ivory-bill suffered more from the ax than from the gun, although certainly direct destruction was not unknown. The Indians coveted his bill for personal adornments, and the shooters of song and garden birds could hardly resist (or miss) so large and handsome a bird as this. Still, though, it was the ax.

The ivory-bill lives only on wood-boring insects, and almost entirely on beetles of three families: Buprestidae, Cerambycidae, and Elateridae. These beetle families, in turn, live in dying or recently dead trees of several kinds. Preferred are the oaks of the genus *Quercus*, the sweetgum *Liquidambar styraciflua*, the cypress *Taxodium distichum*, and the green ash *Fraxinus pennsylvanica*, and it was in those trees that the ivory-billed woodpecker was most often seen. But these trees do best in heavily forested areas, usually on frequently flooded alluvial land bordering on river systems, and it is only in stands of virgin timber that recently dead trees can be found. It was just such trees as these that fell first to timber cutters.

The ivory-bill probably never abounded. His needs were so special that the population almost certainly remained at a practical level. Senile though the species may have been, however, barring man or

a gross climate change it probably could have survived. Remoteness was required, remoteness and virgin timber in well-watered land. Perhaps the mountainous interior of Cuba may yet harbor a few pairs of *carpintero real*, as it is known there. Certainly, if any do remain in the United States (there are none in zoos) they are beyond helping.

Man cannot really be blamed for what happened to this striking woodpecker. The cutting of timber in a newly settled land is surely a legitimate activity. It wasn't until recently, really, that man found out that this important species was on the way out. At that point, however, he should have established preserves and at least tried to help.

If we are to be honest, we must acknowledge that some species are doomed no matter what we do. The ivory-billed woodpecker is such a species. It can be considered a symbol of all the other species we have caused to die out. Everywhere one goes there are tablets and signs telling of battles fought between men, and monuments and memorials to the dead and wounded. Why not also commemorate battles lost by victors and victims alike? Surely, when man sets himself against the land and against its products, plant and animal, he is more the loser the greater his victory. You cannot defy nature and win.

Some Further Thoughts

In a very real sense, the problems discussed in the preceding chapters are not only international in scope, but universal.

Twenty-five years ago we lived in the comfortable assurance that our small planet was the only place in the universe where life existed. A great many comforts have been taken away from us in the last few decades, emotional and intellectual comforts traded in on scientific ones as a down payment on the future. The most profound comfort lost was the assurance of uniqueness.

It is fairly evident to virtually every scientist who has given the matter some thought that life exists on perhaps millions of other planets besides Earth. Our sun, a very ordinary star, is one of approximately 150,000,000,000 stars in our own galaxy, and our galaxy is in fact but one of uncounted billions. There are undoubt-edly billions of planets in the universe where at least the life *condition* exists. We cannot guess what this life is like. In fact, aside from the fact that we live it, we do not know very much about life at all.

We have long assumed, and this is another of those wonderful emotional comforts we took for granted, that man was an ultimate creature. We are what it is all about, we thought. It was all leading *up* to us. One must wonder, since millions of stars are far older than our sun and therefore their planets millions of years older than Earth, what life will be like there when contact is made. What is life like when it has four or five million years longer to evolve? Evolution, after all, has not stopped with us and, as far as any reason can discern, never stops. Man still has an appendix, and still has a little toe although his foot can no longer grasp a limb!

The next century or two may well reveal to us that we are in fact nothing more nor less than a very transient bit of animal life heading for far bigger things. Perhaps other life forms are also headed for bigger things. It appears, unfortunately, that while in this transient stage we have developed enough intelligence to rule, but not enough to use rationally the power that ruling implies.

More explicitly, man has the ability to maintain or destroy other life forms on Earth, but not the judgment to know which to do. If anything is testimony to how early we are in our develop-ment, that fact is. We are children playing with matches. The analogy goes further; children playing with matches often set things on fire and cause senseless and extremely dangerous destruction. What has man been doing if it has not been senseless and dangerous destruction? It is senseless because we have the reasoning powers to know better. It is dangerous on several counts. First, we destroy life yet we don't understand it. Second, we are in dire danger of con-demning all those who follow us to a world raped, sickened, hollow, and resembling nothing so much as a terrible wasteland.

There are those of us who find New York, London, Paris, Rome, and Tokyo beautiful. Surely, they are. They are monuments to skill, still being born, skill developing. But would these cities be beautiful if they and nothing else existed? Is not a city a beautiful thing because man can choose it for a day or a week or a year? If there is one day soon nothing else, if we deny our children the choice, then every city on this Earth will be a prison!

What hell it would be if there were no natural settings. What a disaster for the soul, for the mind, and for our scientific progress if man were all there was! And what guilt would torture our souls. Wildlife is our connection with the real world. It is the bridge to the past and to the future. It is an absolutely invaluable link with life, not only on this planet but on millions of others.

This is not mysticism. This is the reality of the sciences of the future. When the estimate is stretched to the absolute breaking point, our civilization is ten thousand years old. That is a blink, a flash, a mere fraction of a second in time as it is reckoned in this universe. Ten thousand years is not long enough for us to know what we are doing. We are too young, too inexperienced to make judgments such as "Shall there be life other than our own on this planet?" Could there be a more profound question than this? Could any animal species have demonstrated more conclusively their inability to answer such a question than we have? Since we are unable yet to stop killing each other, since we are still blown about by every gust of emotional wind to the point where we shoot at the slightest provocation, how dare we presume to pass judgment on all other life?

In case the statistics that are liberally sprinkled throughout the chapters that have gone before have not made the point, permit me to make it now. Man at this point in history is deciding whether or not he shall share this planet or shall inhabit it alone. He is deciding whether there shall be concrete and steel and nothing else. The difference between the way things are going now and the complete and utter destruction of everything natural on this planet is not a difference in kind, but only in degree. Stepping up the present pace will result in utter desolation.

Francis Harper has given us the following statistics on mammals alone. Between the years A.D. 1 and A.D. 1800, thirty-three known mammalian forms became extinct. That is one mammal killed off essentially by the activity of man every fifty-four and a half years. Between the years A.D. 1801 and A.D. 1850, two mammals at least became extinct. That is a mammal every twenty-five years—a 100 per cent increase!

To carry this unfortunate graph a bit further, between the years A.D. 1851 and A.D. 1900, at least thirty-one mammals were exterminated. That is a mammal every 1.6 years! Between the years A.D. 1901 and A.D. 1944, forty mammalian forms were destroyed. That is nearly an animal a year! From one mammal every fifty-four and a half years to a mammal a year. In addition, at present there are 1000 species in danger at least, including birds, reptiles, and amphibians. In the next few decades *all* of these could go.

Examine for a moment a sample of our contemporary behavior. You may recall some earlier remarks about the feather trade. Lest you think that kind of thing is in the past, note the following facts.

The polar bear is an endangered species, as we have seen. Yet, during the winter 1965–1966, in New York City alone, Abercrombie & Fitch, B. Altman, and Georges Kaplan offered polar bear rugs in newspaper ads. The African cheetah faces extinction yet B. Altman offered women's coats made of cheetah skins. Bonwit Teller offered jaguar coats, and The Tailored Woman offered leopard coats. African lions and tigers from somewhere in Asia were also considered fashionable by these same stores. In London, these skins are also offered, along with wolf, lynx, and many other furs. The New York *Times* noted in December, 1965:

> Certain United States business interests, including some noted retail stores, are currently promoting the sale of rugs, upholstered items, and articles of clothing made of the skins of polar bears, Asian tiger, Brazilian jaguar, and African lion, leopard, and cheetah. This merchandising is contributing substantially to already great pressures on wildlife through hunting and habitat destruction.

Here we have proof positive, in the form of newspaper advertising, that business interests and so-called fashion in ultra-urbane New York City, London, Paris, Rome, and the other major cities of the world are encouraging poachers, despoilers, slaughterers in underprivileged and often naive rural locales. Is this the maturity of a civilization capable of making great judgments on matters of life and death?

Surely we must realize that this is our last chance on Earth. Where can we go after this?

I am convinced that when we finally take our childhood's first step and make contact with life elsewhere than on Earth we will find, very often, life very much more advanced than our own. I do not expect science fiction monsters with all the evil characteristics that have been predicted for them only as projections of our own shortcomings. We will find life that has been able to overcome that with which we are still struggling. These advanced intelligences will have arrived at points we can only dream of achieving. Perhaps, though, when they see what we have done they will become hostile. Perhaps if we can't make the grade here, they will not welcome us anywhere else. Perhaps they will want to confine us to our own living hell, a hell of our own making. This is our last chance to avoid that hell. Will we take it?

Selected Bibliography

THIS LIST represents those references the author personally feels will be of particular use for anyone wishing to further examine the problems discussed in this book. For every one listed here, there are, of course, a dozen more. Nor has any attempt been made to include periodical literature which is a rich if bewilderingly endless source of information on the problems of conservation.

ALLEN, GLOVER M. *Extinct and Vanishing Mammals of the Western Hemisphere.* American Committee for International Wildlife Protection, New York, 1942.

AUSTIN, OLIVER A. *Birds of the World.* The Golden Press, New York, 1961.

BOONE & CROCKETT CLUB. *Records of North American Big Game.* Holt, Rinehart & Winston, New York, 1964.

Selected Bibliography

DELACOUR, JEAN. *The Waterfowl of the World* (4 Vols.) Country Life, Ltd., London, 1964.

DENIS, ARMAND. *Cats of the World.* Houghton, Mifflin Co., Boston, 1964.

ENGELHARDT, WOLFGANG, ed. *Survival of the Free.* Hamish Hamilton, London, 1962.

GEE, E. P. *The Wild Life of India.* E. P. Dutton Co., Ltd., New York, 1964.

GREENWAY, JAMES C., JR. *Extinct and Vanishing Birds of the World.* American Committee for International Wildlife Protection, New York, 1958.

GROSSMAN, MARY LOUISE and JOHN HAMLET. *Birds of Prey of the World.* Clarkson N. Potter, Inc., New York, 1964.

HARPER, FRANCIS. *Extinct and Vanishing Mammals of the Old World.* American Committee for International Wildlife Protection, New York, 1945.

HILSCHER, HERB and MIRIAM. *Alaska, U.S.A.* Little, Brown & Co., Boston, 1959.

INTERNATIONAL UNION FOR CONSERVATION OF NATURE AND NATURAL RESOURCES. *Red Data Book* (2 Vols.) IUCN, Morges, Switzerland, 1966.

KING, JUDITH. *Seals of the World.* British Museum (Natural History), London, 1964.

LAWS, RICHARD M. *Problems of Whale Conservation.* Transactions of the Twenty-Fifth North American Wildlife Conference, Wildlife Management Institute, Washington, D. C., 1960.

MABERLY, C. T. ASTLEY. *The Game Animals of Southern Africa.* Nelson, Cape Town, 1963.

MACKINTOSH, N. A. *The Natural History of Whalebone.* Smithsonian Institution, Washington, D. C., 1947.

MATTHIESSEN, PETER. *Wildlife in America.* Viking Press, New York, 1959.

ORMOND, CLYDE. *Bear!* The Stackpole Co., Harrisburg, 1961.

SCHALLER, GEORGE B. *The Mountain Gorilla.* The University of Chicago Press, Chicago, 1963.

SCHEFFER, VICTOR B. *Seals, Sea Lions and Walruses.* Stanford University Press, Stanford, 1958.

SCHMIDT, KARL P. and ROBERT F. INGER. *Living Reptiles of the World.* Hanover House, New York, 1957.

SCOTT, PETER, ed. *The Launching of a New Ark.* World Wildlife Fund, London, 1965.

Selected Bibliography

SMITH, DICK and ROBERT EASTON. *California Condor: Vanishing American.* McNally Loftin, Charlotte/Santa Barbara, 1964.

SPINAGE, C. A. *Animals of East Africa.* Collins, London, 1962.

STREET, PHILIP. *Vanishing Animals.* E. P. Dutton & Co. Inc., New York, 1961.

THOMSON, SIR A. LANDSBOROUGH, ed. *A New Dictionary of Birds.* McGraw-Hill Co., New York, 1964.

TRIPPENSEE, REUBEN EDWIN. *Wildlife Management* (2 Vols.) McGraw-Hill Co., New York, 1948.

TROUGHTON, ELLIS. *Furred Animals of Australia.* Chas. Scribner's Sons, New York, 1947.

WALKER, ERNEST P., et al. *Mammals of the World* (2 Vols.) The Johns Hopkins Press, Baltimore, 1964.

ZOOLOGICAL SOCIETY OF LONDON. *The International Zoo Yearbook* (Vol. 1: 1959; Vol. 2: 1960; Vol. 3: 1961; Vol. 4: 1962; Vol. 5: 1965). Zoological Society of London, London.

Appendices

CONSERVATION ORGANIZATIONS

FOR THOSE READERS who are not satisfied with feeling bad about something, but who want to join in a worldwide effort to correct it, the following list is provided. It is an abbreviated list of organizations in the United States involved in conservation work. Most of these organizations need funds, workers, and help in general. Add to this list the state departments responsible within the individual states and you have a good starting place for your enthusiasm and support.

AFRICAN WILDLIFE LEADERSHIP
FOUNDATION
1717 Massachusetts Avenue
N.W.
Washington, D.C. 20036

AMERICAN CETACEAN SOCIETY
4725 Lincoln Boulevard
Marina Del Rey, California
90291

AMERICAN FISHERIES SOCIETY
Washington Building
15th and New York Avenue
Washington, D.C. 20005

THE AMERICAN FORESTRY ASSOCIATION
1319 18th Street N.W.
Washington, D.C. 20036

DEFENDERS OF WILDLIFE
2000 N Street N.W.
Washington, D.C. 20036

DUCKS UNLIMITED, INC.
P.O. Box 66300
Chicago, Illinois 60666

ELSA WILD ANIMAL APPEAL
P.O. Box 1244
San Clemente, California 92672

FRIENDS OF THE EARTH
30 East 42nd Street
New York, New York 10022

THE GARDEN CLUB OF AMERICA
598 Madison Avenue
New York, New York 10022

HUMANE SOCIETY OF THE UNITED STATES
1604 K Street N.W.
Washington, D.C. 20006

THE IZAAK WALTON LEAGUE OF AMERICA
1800 North Kent Street
Arlington, Virginia 22209

NATIONAL AUDUBON SOCIETY
950 Third Avenue
New York, New York 10022

NATIONAL WILDLIFE FEDERATION
1412 Sixteenth Street N.W.
Washington, D.C. 20036

THE NATURE CONSERVANCY
1800 North Kent Street
Arlington, Virginia 22209

NEW YORK ZOOLOGICAL SOCIETY
Bronx, New York 10460

SIERRA CLUB
1050 Mills Tower
San Francisco, California 94104

THE WILDERNESS SOCIETY
729 15th Street N.W.
Washington, D.C. 20005

THE WILDLIFE MANAGEMENT INSTITUTE
709 Wire Building
Washington, D.C. 20005

WORLD WILDLIFE FUND
1910 17th Street N.W.
Washington, D.C. 20006

The following conservation creed by one of the world's foremost experts in the field, the naturalist and painter, Peter Scott, is worthy of reproduction here. Permission for its use was granted by the World Wildlife Fund in London.

A VOICE CRYING IN THE WILDERNESS?

WHAT man did to the Dodo, and has since been doing to the Blue Whale and about 1,000 other kinds of animals, may or may not be morally wrong. But the conservation of nature is most important because of what nature does for man.

I believe something goes wrong with man when he cuts himself off from the natural world. I think he knows it, and this is why he keeps gardens and window-boxes and house plants, and dogs and cats and budgerigars. Man does not live by bread alone. I believe he should take just as great pains to look after the natural treasures which inspire him as he does to preserve his man-made treasures in art galleries and museums. This is a responsibility we have to future generations, just as we are responsible for the safeguarding of Westminster Abbey or the Mona Lisa.

It has been argued that if the human population of the world continues to increase at its present rate, there will soon be no room for either wildlife or wild places, so why waste time, effort and money trying to conserve them now? But I believe that sooner or later man will learn to limit his own over-population. Then he will become much more widely concerned with optimum rather than maximum, quality rather than quantity, and will rediscover the need within himself for contact with wilderness and wild nature.

No one can tell when this will happen. I am concerned that when it does, breeding stocks of wild animals and plants should still exist, preserved perhaps mainly in nature reserves and national parks, even in zoos and botanical gardens, from which to re-populate the natural environment man will then wish to recreate and rehabilitate.

These are my reasons for believing passionately in the conservation of nature.

All this calls for action of three kinds: more research in ecology, the setting aside of more land as effectively inviolate strongholds, and above all education. By calling attention to the plight of the world's wildlife, and by encouraging people to enrich their lives by the enjoyment of nature, it may be possible to accelerate both the change in outlook and the necessary action.

It has been estimated that conservation all over the world needs each year £2 million. This is no astronomical figure. It is half the price of a V bomber, less than one twelfth the price of the new Cunarder, or the price of, say, three or four world-famous paintings.

Much money is needed for relieving human suffering, but some is also needed for human fulfilment and inspiration. Conservation, like education and art, claims some proportion of the money we give to help others, including the as yet unborn.

Even if I am wrong about the long-term prospects—if man were to fail to solve his own over-population problem, and reaches the stage 530 years hence when there will be standing room only on this earth—even then the conservation effort will have been worth while. It will have retained at least for a time, some of the natural wonders. Measured in man-hours of enjoyment and inspiration this alone would be worth the effort. Many will have enjoyed the pictures even if the gallery is burnt down in the end.

The community chest which seeks to make the gallery representative and maintains the fire-alarm system is The World Wildlife Fund.

A conservation creed by
PETER SCOTT
Chairman of the
World Wildlife Fund

ROGER A. CARAS

Unlike the animals he studies, Roger A. Caras has no limited natural habitat. Born in 1928 in Methuen, Massachusetts, he has traveled to the South Pole, crossed the Pacific twelve times and the Atlantic more times than he can count.

His life itinerary also is incredibly varied. He studied cinema at the University of Southern California, theater at Tufts College and zoology at Northeastern University. He has acted on television, written screenplays, run a story department for Broadway producers, trained dogs, taken care of monkeys, driven cabs, dug for archeological remnants, and lectured on film history and conservation. He worked for Columbia Pictures once and the Army twice. Mr. Caras also skindives, rides in submarines, and photographs wild animals.

Finally, Mr. Caras is an author. *Last Chance on Earth* is his third book for Chilton. *Antarctica: Land of Frozen Time*, his first work, was inspired by his trek over the icy continent. Thousands more readers were introduced to Mr. Caras through *Dangerous to Man*, which authoritatively distinguished animals which are killers in fact from those which kill in fiction only.

CHARLES FRACÉ

As an artist and photographer, Mr. Fracé has specialized in the study of animals. He has collected for his household an impressive variety of wildlife forms—snakes, mammals, and birds—and continues to take frequent field trips to capture even more species on film and paper.